Illustrated Bhagavad Gita for Kids

Published by
GRAPEVINE BOOKS

www.grapevinebooks.com
email: contact@grapevinebooks.com
Ordering Information:
Quantity sales: Special discounts are available on quantity purchases
by corporations, associations, and others.
For details, reach out to the publisher.

First published by Grapevine Books 2025

How to Read This Book

This book brings the wisdom of the **Bhagavad Gita** to life through simple conversations between a curious child and his Guruji.

Each shloka (verse) is spread across two pages.

After reading each shloka, take your time to think about what you learnt. If something feels new or confusing, that's okay. Remember, you're here to learn and grow!

You can read this book by yourself or with someone older. Ask questions, share your thoughts, and enjoy the journey.

Adhyaya 1

The Bhagavad Gita begins with Sanjaya narrating to the blind King Dhrtarastra, the scene of the battlefield of **Kuruksetra**, wherein assembled are two armies - one headed by the five Pandava brothers representing *dharma* [righteousness] and the other headed by the sons of Dhrtarasta representing *adharma* [unrighteousness]. **Arjuna**, the leading Pandava, requests his chariot-driver and friend, **Krishna** to take his chariot in between the two armies so that he could closely inspect those who have come to combat them.

Induced by Krishna, Arjuna experiences an acute weakness of heart upon seeing his own family members on the combating side.

Arjuna is torn between his duty as a warrior and his emotional attachments to his family, friends, and teachers who are on the opposing side of the battle. His inner conflict intensifies, leading him to question the righteousness of the war.

Filled with doubt and distress, Arjuna turns to Lord Krishna, **seeking guidance**. He expresses his inner turmoil and moral dilemmas, indicating that he would rather renounce the battle than engage in such a conflict.

Arjuna's state of mind allows Lord Krishna to impart timeless wisdom, which becomes the foundation for the transformative teachings in the subsequent adhyayas.

Guruji, I'm facing a big dilemma. There's a crucial examination approaching, and I feel lost and unsure about how to prepare.
It's good that you've come to me, dear child. Remember these words from the Bhagavad Gita

Kārpaṇyadoṣopahatasvabhāvaḥ,
Pṛcchāmi tvāṁ dharmasammūḍhacetāḥ |
Yacchreyaḥ syānniścitaṁ brūhi tanme,
śiṣyaste'haṁ śādhi māṁ tvāṁ prapannam || 7 ||
I am confused about my duty, and am besieged with anxiety and faintheartedness. I am Your disciple, and am surrendered to You. Please instruct me for certain what is best for me.

This shloka reminds us of the value of seeking guidance when we're uncertain about our path. Just as Arjuna turned to Krishna for guidance on the battlefield, you can approach your teachers, mentors, and even your parents. They hold the wisdom that can illuminate your path.
But Guruji, won't it be bothersome for them? They already have so much to do.
Seeking knowledge is never a bother, dear child. The shloka assure us that seeking guidance leads to surety. Your mentors and guides will be glad to help you. It's a gesture of respect for their knowledge.
You're right, Guruji. I will gather the courage to seek help and guidance. But what if they ask me why I'm feeling this way?
Honest communication is the key, my child. Explain your concerns, just as Arjuna revealed his doubts to Krishna.
Remember, seeking guidance is a way to grow and learn.

Guruji, I'm really worried about my aunt. She's been very sick, and I don't know what to do.
I'm sorry to hear about your aunt's illness, my dear. But remember what the Bhagavad Gita teaches us.

Shrī Bhagavān uvācha |
Ashocyānanvashocastvaṁ prajñāvādānśhcha bhāṣhase |
Gatāsūnagatāsūṁśhcha nānuśhochanti paṇḍitāḥ || 11 ||
While you speak words of wisdom, you are mourning for that which is not worthy of grief. The wise lament neither for the living nor for the dead.

Wise people neither lament for the living, nor the dead. Your concern for your aunt is a sign of empathy and care. While it's important to be there for your aunt and your family, it's also crucial to keep a broader perspective.
BHAGAVAD GITA
But Guruji, how can I not feel sad when someone I care about is suffering?
It's natural to feel sad, my dear. But wisdom lies in understancing the impermanence of life. Instead of focusing solely on the present difficulties, try to see the bigger picture - the cycles of life and the resilience that comes along.
I'm just afraid of losing her, Guruji.
Your feelings are valid, but remember that life is a journey with its ups and downs.
Wise people channel their emotions to uplift themselves and others. You can offer your support to your aunt and your family while also finding strength within to cope with challenges.

Guruji, my aunt was admitted to the hospital last night. I visited her today, and it was really hard to see her like that
I understand, my dear. It's never easy to see our loved ones facing health challenges. But remember the teachings of the Bhagavad Gita.

Na tvevāhaṁ jātu nāsaṁ na tvaṁ neme janādhipāḥ |
Na chaiva na bhaviṣhyāmaḥ sarve vayamataḥ param || 12 ||
Never was there a time when I did not exist, nor you, nor all these kings; nor in the future shall any of us cease to be.

It means that the soul is eternal and has no lasting existence. Just as there was never a time when Krishna, Arjuna, or any of the kings didn't exist, the same holds for all of us. Our souls have neither birth nor death.
So you're saying that even if her body is weak now, her soul will always be strong?

Exactly. The physical body may change, but the soul remains unchanging and immortal. The memories you share with your aunt will remain, even if circumstances change. Understanding the eternal nature of the soul can help you find strength in knowing that the essence of who she is will always be with you.
I guess you're right, Guruji. I'll try to focus on the happy memories we've had and cherish the time I have with her.

Guruji, I just got news that my aunt passed away. I'm feeling really sad and lost.
I'm so sorry to hear that, my dear. Losing a loved one is never easy. But remember the teachings of the Bhagavad Gita.

dehino 'smin yathā dehe kaumāraṁ yauvanaṁ jarā
tathā dehāntara-prāptir dhīras tatra na muhyati
|| 13 ||
Just as the embodied soul continuously passes from childhood to youth to old age, similarly, at the time of death, the soul passes into another body. The wise are not deluded by this.

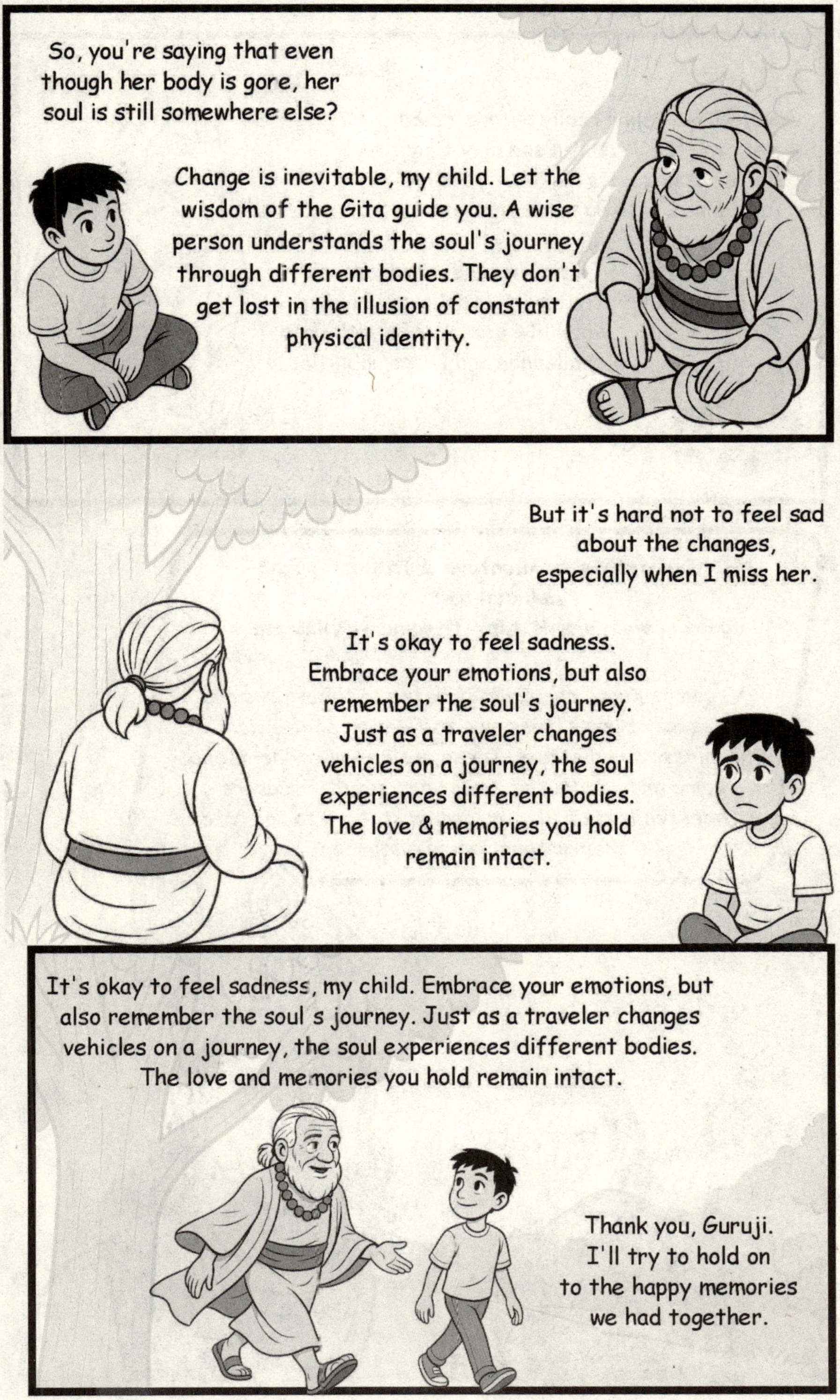
So, you're saying that even though her body is gore, her soul is still somewhere else?
Change is inevitable, my child. Let the wisdom of the Gita guide you. A wise person understands the soul's journey through different bodies. They don't get lost in the illusion of constant physical identity.
But it's hard not to feel sad about the changes, especially when I miss her.
It's okay to feel sadness. Embrace your emotions, but also remember the soul's journey. Just as a traveler changes vehicles on a journey, the soul experiences different bodies. The love & memories you hold remain intact.
It's okay to feel sadness, my child. Embrace your emotions, but also remember the soul's journey. Just as a traveler changes vehicles on a journey, the soul experiences different bodies. The love and memories you hold remain intact.
Thank you, Guruji. I'll try to hold on to the happy memories we had together.

Guruji, I'm feeling really overwhelmed lately, my family is still sad about my aunt's passing. It's hard to focus on academics with so much going on.
I understand, my dear. It's natural to feel overwhelmed when life presents us with both challenges and responsibilities.
mātrā-sparśhās tu kaunteya śhītoṣhṇa-sukha-duḥkha-dāḥ
āgamāpāyino 'nityās tāns-titikṣhasva bhārata
|| 14 ||
O son of Kunti, the contact between the senses and the sense objects gives rise to fleeting perceptions of happiness and distress. These are non-permanent, and come and go like the winter and summer seasons. O descendent of Bharat, one must learn to tolerate them without being disturbed.

It means that the experiences we have in life - whether they bring happiness or sadness - are temporary and fleeting, much like the changing seasons of winter and summer. Just as winter and summer come and go, so do our feelings of joy and sorrow. They are not permanent.
But it's so hard to ignore the sadness and focus on my studies.
It's okay to acknowledge your emotions and be there for your family. But it's also important to remember that these emotions are like passing clouds. They come and go. What's important is to not get disturbed by them.
How do I do that, Guruji?
It takes practice, my dear. When you find yourself getting overwhelmed, take a deep breath and remind yourself that these emotions are temporary. Focus on the task at hand, whether it's your studies or supporting your family. With time, you'll develop the strength to face life's challenges.
So, you're saying that I should learn to endure these ups and downs without letting them affect me too much?
Exactly, my dear.
Life will always have its share of joys and sorrows.
By developing the ab lity to tolerate them with a steady mind,
you'll not only navigate through difficult times effectively,
but also maintain your focus and balance.

Guruji, my mother has been really sad lately. Whenever she thinks about my aunt's passing, she starts crying. I want to help her feel better, but I don't know how.
Grief is a natural emotion when we lose someone we care about. It's important to be there for your mother during this time. Here's a shloka from Gita that might help.

na jāyate mriyate vā kadāchin nāyaṁ bhūtvā bhavitā vā na bhūyaḥ ajo nityaḥ śhāśhvato 'yaṁ purāṇo na hanyate hanyamāne śharīre
The soul is neither born, nor does it ever die; nor having once existed, does it ever cease to be. The soul is without birth, eternal, immortal, and ageless. It is not destroyed when the body is destroyed.

Your mother's sadness is a natural expression of her love and connection with your aunt. Just like you miss her, your mother also misses her presence. It's okay for her to feel sad, and it's important for her to grieve in her own way.

Guruji, I visited my aunt's house yesterday, and it made me so sad. Everything reminded me of her, and I realized she's really gone.
It's natural to feel sad when we are reminded of our loved ones who have passed away. The connection we had with them is deeply engraved in our hearts. But let the teachings of the Bhagavad Gita guide you through these difficult times.
vāsānsi jīrṇāni yathā vihāya
navāni gṛihṇāti naro 'parāṇi
tathā śharīrāṇi vihāya jīrṇānya
nyāni sanyāti navāni dehī || 22 ||
As a person sheds worn-out garments and wears new ones, likewise, at the time of death, the soul casts off its worn-out body and enters a new one.
Just as we discard old and worn-out clothes for new ones, the soul leaves behind its old body and takes on a new one in the cycle of rebirth.
So, you're saying that even though my aunt's physical body is gone, her soul is still there somewhere?
Yes, my dear. The soul is eternal and immortal. While the physical body changes and eventually ceases to exist, the essence of who we are continues on. Remember, change is a part of life.

How do I cope with these feelings of sadness, Guruji?

Sadness is a natural part of the process. But also, try to focus on the beautiful memories you shared with your aunt and the love that continues to live on within you.
Just like you change clothes when they become old, life also presents us with new chapters and new experiences to embrace.

Guruji, I've been thinking a lot lately. I saw how my aunt passed away, and it made me worry about my mom. What if something happens to her too?
It's natural to feel concerned about the people we love. But remember that worrying about the future won't change it. Here's a shloka from Bhagavad Gita that might offer you some guidance.

nainaṁ chhindanti śhastrāṇi nainaṁ dahati pāvakaḥ
na chainaṁ kledayantyāpo na śhoṣhayati mārutaḥ
|| 23 ||
Weapons cannot shred the soul, nor can fire burn it. Water cannot wet it, nor can the wind dry it.

It means that the soul can't be harmed by any physical means. The soul is eternal and beyond the reach of physical harm
So, you're saying that my mom's soul is safe and can't be harmed?

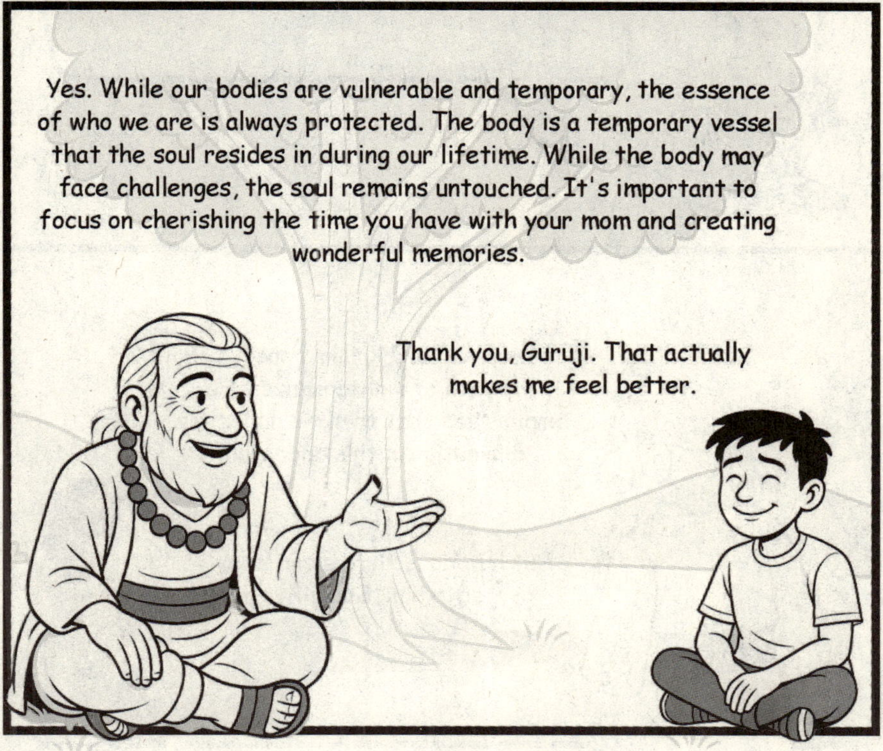
Yes. While our bodies are vulnerable and temporary, the essence of who we are is always protected. The body is a temporary vessel that the soul resides in during our lifetime. While the body may face challenges, the soul remains untouched. It's important to focus on cherishing the time you have with your mom and creating wonderful memories.
Thank you, Guruji. That actually makes me feel better.

Guruji, I'm really worried about my upcoming exams. After my aunt's passing, I took quite a few leaves from school to be with my family. Now I feel like I'm so far behind in my studies, and the exams are just around the corner.
I understand your concern, my dear. It's natural to feel overwhelmed, especially when facing academic challenges alongside personal ones. But let me remind you of a shloka from Bhagavad Gita.
nehābhikrama-nāśho 'sti pratyavāyo na vidyate svalpam apyasya dharmasya trāyate mahato bhayāt || 40 ||
Working in this state of consciousness, there is no loss or adverse result, and even a little effort saves one from great danger.
In the shloka Lord Krishna speaks about the path of righteousness. He emphasizes that there is no loss or diminution in this endeavor.
But how does that apply to my situation, Guruji?

Every bit of effort you put into your studies, no matter how small it might seem, is valuable. Even a little progress on this path can protect you from the fear of failure. It's not about comparing yourself to others or worrying about how much time you lost.
So, you mean even if I've missed some days of studying, it's still worth trying my best?

Absolutely, my dear. Life is full of challenges and interruptions, but what counts is how you respond to them. Instead of dwelling on what you couldn't do, focus on what you can do now. Remember that your effort and determination matter more than the obstacles you faced.

Guruji, I've been thinking about joining the school's Table Tennis club to take a break from studies in the evenings. But at the same time, I also want to participate in the Debate Club. I'm so confused about what to do!
Let me share a verse from the Bhagavad Gita that might offer you some insight.

vyavasāyātmikā buddhir ekeha kuru-nandana bahu-śhākhā hyanantāśh cha buddhayo 'vyavasāyinām || 41 ||
O descendent of the Kurus, the intellect of those who are on this path is resolute, and their aim is one-pointed. But the intellect of those who are irresolute is many-branched.

Exploring interests is wonderful, my child. The Gita's teachings can help you make informed decisions. It says the intellect of the irresolute is many-branched, while the focused intellect is one-pointed.
So, you're saying that I should just stick to one thing and ignore all the other interests?
Not exactly, dear one. It's about finding a balance between exploring different interests and maintaining focus. Just as a tree with many branches can lead to scattered energy, a one-pointed approach can yield better results.
But Guruji, I'm afraid that if I choose one interest, I might miss out on the others.
Balancing interests requires wisdom, my child. The Gita's teachings guide us to cultivate a one-pointed approach while appreciating exploration. When you're torn between options, remind yourself of your ultimate goal.
Begin by acknowledging your interests without letting them cloud your focus.

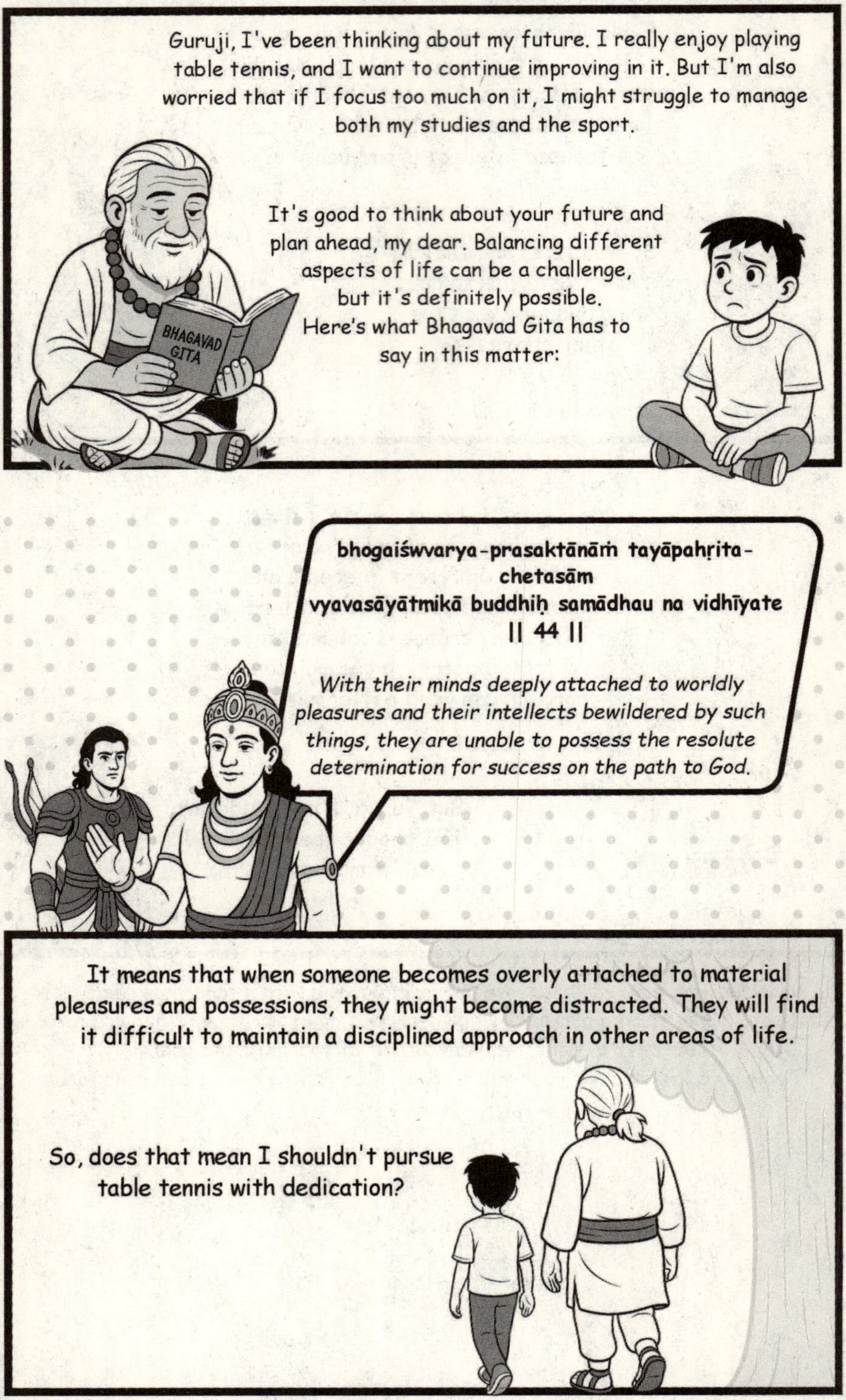
Guruji, I've been thinking about my future. I really enjoy playing table tennis, and I want to continue improving in it. But I'm also worried that if I focus too much on it, I might struggle to manage both my studies and the sport.
It's good to think about your future and plan ahead, my dear. Balancing different aspects of life can be a challenge, but it's definitely possible. Here's what Bhagavad Gita has to say in this matter:
BHAGAVAD GITA
bhogaiśwvarya-prasaktānāṁ tayāpahṛita-chetasām
vyavasāyātmikā buddhiḥ samādhau na vidhīyate
|| 44 ||
With their minds deeply attached to worldly pleasures and their intellects bewildered by such things, they are unable to possess the resolute determination for success on the path to God.
It means that when someone becomes overly attached to material pleasures and possessions, they might become distracted. They will find it difficult to maintain a disciplined approach in other areas of life.
So, does that mean I shouldn't pursue table tennis with dedication?

Not at all. Pursuing your passions and interests is important. However, it's essential to strike a balance. Just like you practice table tennis to improve your skills, you also need to practice managing your time and priorities. Decide to excel in both your studies and your sport.
How can I do that, Guruji?

First, set clear goals for yourself in both areas. Create a study schedule with that allocates time for your studies and also for practicing table tennis without neglecting one over the other. Learning to be disciplined and wise with your will not only help you excel in your studies and sports but also cevelop important life skills.
Thank you, Guruji. I feel more confident now about managing both my studies and my passion for table tennis in the future.

Guruji, I've been studying day and night for my upcoming exams, but what if all this hard work doesn't pay off? I'm scared that despite my efforts, I won't get the marks I want.
I understand your concerns, my child. It's natural to feel this way when you've invested so much time and effort. But remember the profound wisdom of the shloka Lord Krishna shared.
karmaṇy-evādhikāras te mā phaleṣhu kadāchana
mā karma-phala-hetur bhūr mā te saṅgo 'stvakarmaṇi || 47 ||
You have a right to perform your prescribed duties, but you are not entitled to the fruits of your actions. Never consider yourself to be the cause of the results of your activities, nor be attached to inaction.
Your ambitions are commendable, but you must also understand the essence of the shloka. It's about performing your duties without getting attached to the outcomes. You have the right to work diligently, but the results are not entirely in your hands.
But if I don't score well, my dreams might shatter. I'll disappoint my parents and myself.

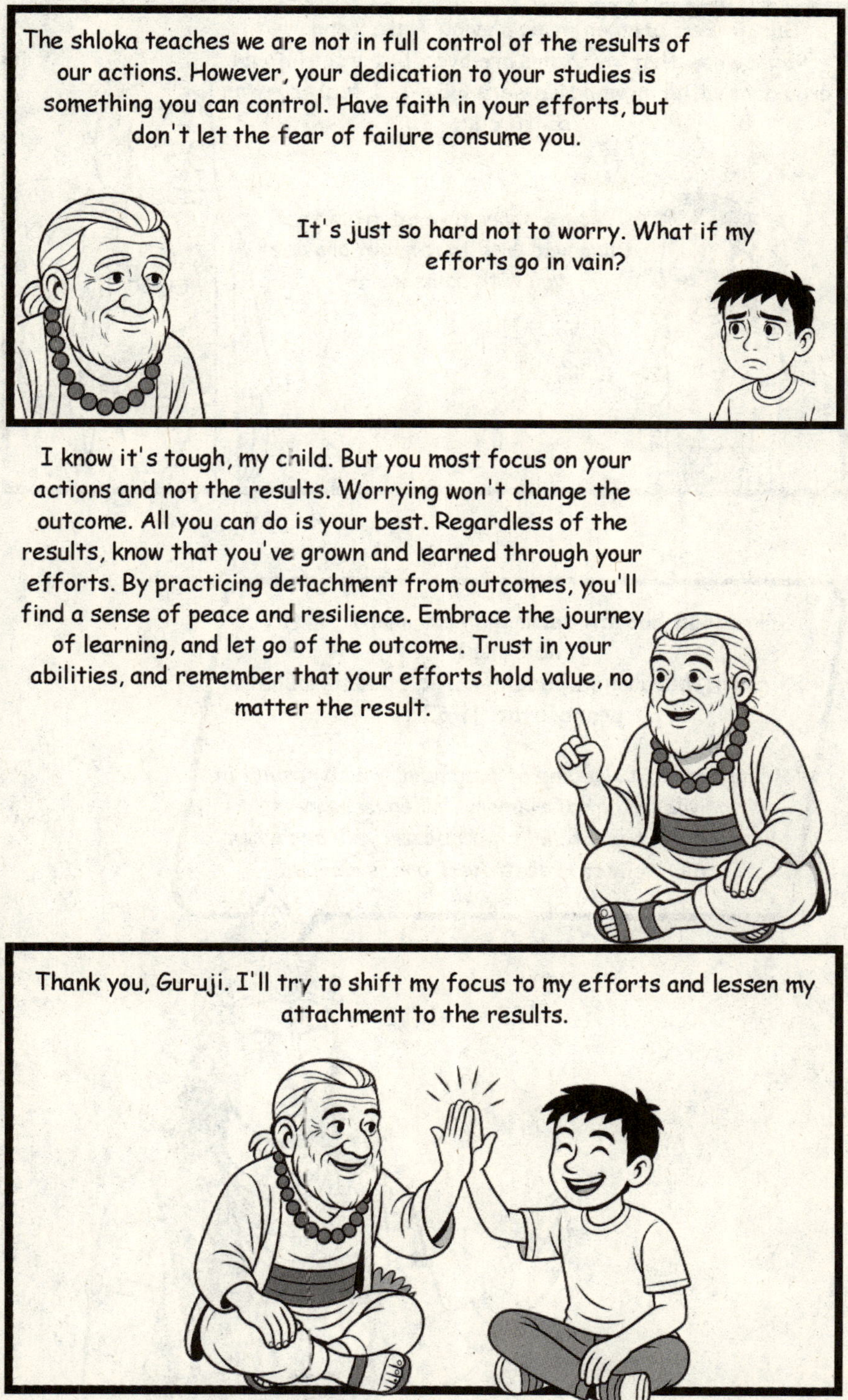
The shloka teaches we are not in full control of the results of our actions. However, your dedication to your studies is something you can control. Have faith in your efforts, but don't let the fear of failure consume you.
It's just so hard not to worry. What if my efforts go in vain?
I know it's tough, my child. But you most focus on your actions and not the results. Worrying won't change the outcome. All you can do is your best. Regardless of the results, know that you've grown and learned through your efforts. By practicing detachment from outcomes, you'll find a sense of peace and resilience. Embrace the journey of learning, and let go of the outcome. Trust in your abilities, and remember that your efforts hold value, no matter the result.
Thank you, Guruji. I'll try to shift my focus to my efforts and lessen my attachment to the results.

Guruji, I've been enjoying playing Table Tennis with Raghav now that my exams are over. But I got into an argument with him while we were playing. I feel angry and confused.
Let me share a verse from the Bhagavad Gita that might provide you with some insight.

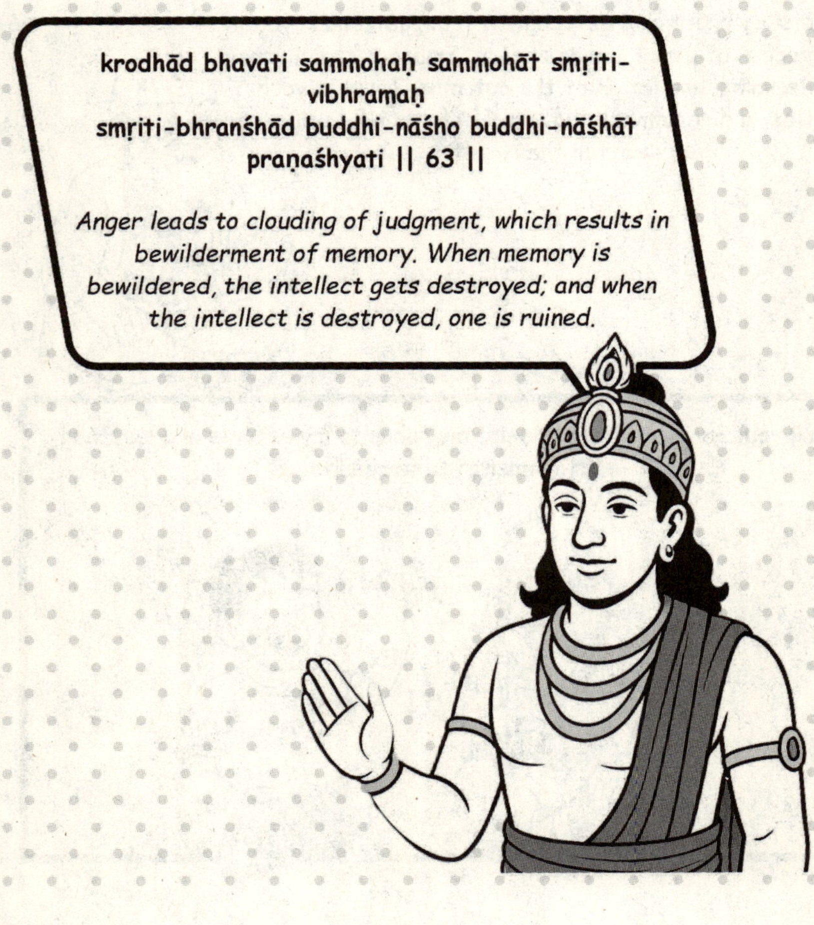
krodhād bhavati sammohaḥ sammohāt smṛiti-vibhramaḥ
smṛiti-bhranśhād buddhi-nāśho buddhi-nāśhāt praṇaśhyati || 63 ||
Anger leads to clouding of judgment, which results in bewilderment of memory. When memory is bewildered, the intellect gets destroyed; and when the intellect is destroyed, one is ruined.

When we let anger cloud our judgment, it can lead to confusion and affect our ability to make wise decisions.
So, you're saying that my anger might be affecting my ability to think clearly and find a solution?
Exactly, my child. When we allow anger to take over, it can make us lose sight of finding a peaceful solution. It's like being caught in a fog of confusion.
But Guruji, how can I overcome this anger and find a way to resolve the situation with Raghav?
Begin by taking a deep breath and acknowledging your feelings without judgment. When you notice anger rising, remind yourself that it's a natural emotion, but it shouldn't control your actions.
Thank you, Guruji. I'll try to remember that while anger is a natural response, I should use it as a catalyst to find a way to resolve conflicts peacefully.

Guruji, the results are out, and I stood second in the class. While I'm glad about it, a part of me wishes I had secured the first rank.
Let me share a verse from the Bhagavad Gita that might offer you some perspective.
āpūryamāṇam achala-pratiṣhṭhaṁ
samudram āpaḥ praviśhanti yadvat
tadvat kāmā yaṁ praviśhanti sarve
sa śhāntim āpnoti na kāma-kāmī || 70 ||
Just as the ocean remains undisturbed by the incessant flow of waters from rivers merging into it, likewise the sage who is unmoved despite the flow of desirable objects all around him attains peace, and not the person who strives to satisfy desires.
The shloka emphasizes finding peace amidst the flow of desires and objects around us. Just like the ocean remains undisturbed despite the merging rivers, a calm mind can find contentment regardless of the outcomes.
I get that, Guruji. But what if I could get a few more marks? I mean, if my teacher could just give me a few extra marks.

My child, seeking more than you have is a natural impulse, but it can lead to restlessness. The one who seeks contentment within attains true peace. Trying to fulfill every desire can create a never-ending cycle of wanting more.
But Guruji, it's just a few marks. It won't hurt anyone.

A few marks might seem insignificant., But the attitude of always seeking more can cloud your mind and prevent you from finding true happiness. True peace comes from learning to appreciate and be content with what you have.
I suppose you're right, Guruji. I'll be content with what I have.

Adhyaya 3
Guruji, I'm going to be a big brother soon! I'm excited, but also a bit nervous about it. I'm worried about having to handle the baby. What if I can't do it properly?
Let me share a verse from the Bhagavad Gita that might offer you guidance.
BHAGAVAD GITA
yajñārthāt karmaṇo 'nyatra loko 'yaṁ karma-bandhanaḥ
tad-arthaṁ karma kaunteya mukta-saṅgaḥ samāchara || 9 ||
Work must be done as a yajna to the Supreme Lord; otherwise, work causes bondage in this material world. Therefore, O son of Kunti, for the satisfaction of God, perform your prescribed duties, without being attached to the results.
Change can bring both excitement and uncertainty, my child. Just like Lord Krishna said, perform your duties as a big brother with the spirit of sacrifice and love. Offer your help, your time, and your care to your new sibling and family.
Yes, Guruji. I know I should help and support my family without expecting anything in return. But it's a big change, and I'm not sure how things will be.

I want to help, Guruji. I want to play with my sibling, help my parents, and be responsible. But what if I make mistakes or things don't go as planned?
Remember, my child, the shloka teaches us to focus on the actions, not the outcomes. Your intention to be a loving and caring big brother is what truly matters. Mistakes are a part of learning and growing. Your willingness to take on this new role will have a positive impact.

I'll try my best, Guruji. It's just that sometimes I feel a bit overwhelmed with all the changes.
It's completely normal to feel that way, my child. Being a big brother is a journey of discovery and growth. Embrace it with patience and kindness towards yourself. Let your actions be driven by love and a sense of duty, and you'll create beautiful memories and bonds that will last a lifetime.

Guruji, my parents have been really busy taking care of the new baby. They haven't had proper meals, and I'm worried about them.
It's wonderful that you're concerned about your parents' well-being, dear child. Let me share a verse from the Bhagavad Gita that might offer you guidance.

annād bhavanti bhūtāni parjanyād anna-sambhavaḥ
yajñād bhavati parjanyo yajñaḥ karma-samudbhavaḥ || 14 ||
All living beings subsist on food, and food is produced by rains. Rains come from the performance of sacrifice, and sacrifice is produced by the performance of prescribed duties.

You can serve your parents by offering them a meal. Your simple act of serving them food can provide them with a moment to rest and recharge. Remember, even small acts of kindness hold great value. When we act with selflessness and care, it contributes to the well-being of the family. This simple act is a form of sacrifice that nurtures the family bond.

Thank you, Guruji. I'll make sure to serve them with love and care.

Guruji, something interesting happened today! I was reading a book to my baby brother, just like Mom does sometimes. He watched me the whole time and even made little sounds like he was reading!
That's wonderful, my young friend! It sounds like you've become quite a role model for your baby brother.
BHAGAVAD GITA
A role model? What's that?
A role model is someone whose actions inspire and influence others in a positive way. Let me share a shloka from the Bhagavad Gita that explains this.
yad yad ācharati śhreṣhṭhas tat tad evetaro janaḥ
sa yat pramāṇaṁ kurute lokas tad anuvartate
|| 21 ||
Whatever actions great persons perform, common people follow. Whatever standards they set, all the world

This shloka speaks of how the actions of great people inspire others to follow their path. Your actions have shown him that reading aloud is a fun and interesting activity.
Wow, that's amazing! I want to be a good role model for him.
You're already on the right path, my dear. Your actions of love, care, and sharing are influencing him positively.
And when I m kind to him, he learns to be kind too?
Precisely. Just as you learn from your parents and other great people, your baby brother is learning from you. Your behaviour sets an example for him to follow.
I'll be the best role model I can be for him!

Guruji, I have a problem. My baby brother started playing with my toys, and I got really possessive about them. I wanted to keep them only for myself.
It's natural to feel that way sometimes, my young friend. Possessiveness is a common emotion. But let me share a shloka from the Bhagavad Gita with you.
prakṛiteḥ kriyamāṇāni guṇaiḥ karmāṇi sarvaśhaḥ
ahankāra-vimūḍhātmā kartāham iti manyate || 27 ||
All activities are carried out by the three modes of material nature. But in ignorance, the soul, deluded by false identification with the body, thinks of itself as the doer.
Material nature can influence our thoughts and emotions, making us feel possessive about things that we consider "ours." But we must remember that everything in the world, including our possessions, is interconnected and part of nature's play.
So, those toys are not only mine?

That's right. The toys have come from the material nature, and they're meant to be enjoyed and shared by everyone. When you share your toys with your baby brother, you're participating in the beautiful circle of sharing and kindness.
I want to share my toys with my baby brother now.

That's a wonderful decision, my dear. When you share, you create joy not only for your baby brother but for yourself as well. Remember, sharing is a way of spreading love and kindness, and it enriches the bond between siblings.

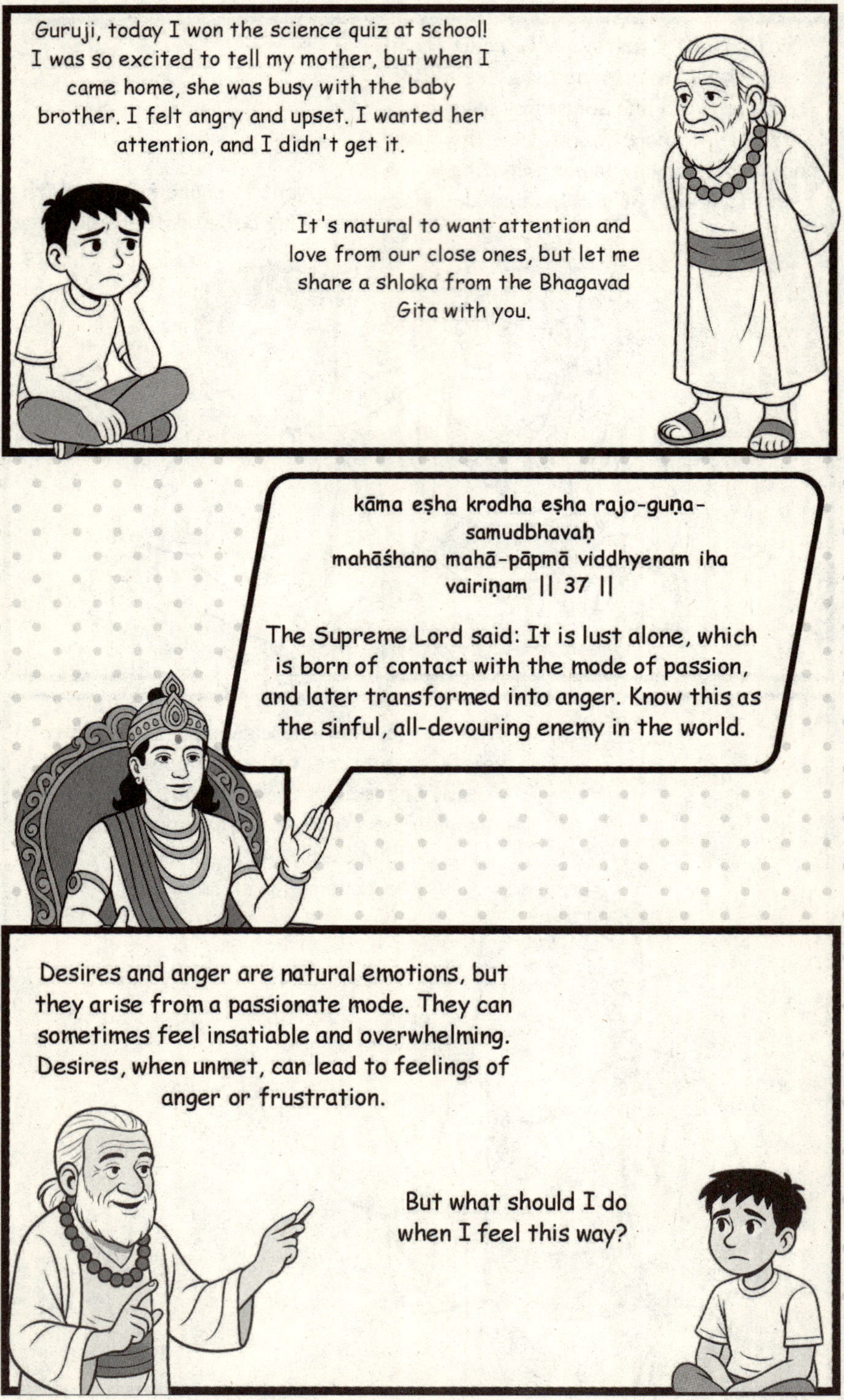
Guruji, today I won the science quiz at school! I was so excited to tell my mother, but when I came home, she was busy with the baby brother. I felt angry and upset. I wanted her attention, and I didn't get it.
It's natural to want attention and love from our close ones, but let me share a shloka from the Bhagavad Gita with you.
kāma eṣha krodha eṣha rajo-guṇa-samudbhavaḥ
mahāśhano mahā-pāpmā viddhyenam iha vairiṇam || 37 ||
The Supreme Lord said: It is lust alone, which is born of contact with the mode of passion, and later transformed into anger. Know this as the sinful, all-devouring enemy in the world.
Desires and anger are natural emotions, but they arise from a passionate mode. They can sometimes feel insatiable and overwhelming. Desires, when unmet, can lead to feelings of anger or frustration.
But what should I do when I feel this way?

In a way, yes. When they control us, they can lead to actions that we might later regret. It's important to recognize these emotions , and to channel them positively. Instead of seeing them as enemies, view them as indicators of how you're feeling and use that knowledge to make choices that reflect your values and goals.

Adhyaya 4
Guruji, I really dislike History lessons at school. It just seems so boring to me. But my Grandfather always insists that I should study History. He says it's important.
Your Grandfather is a wise man. Let me tell you a shloka from the Bhagavad Gita, which might help you.

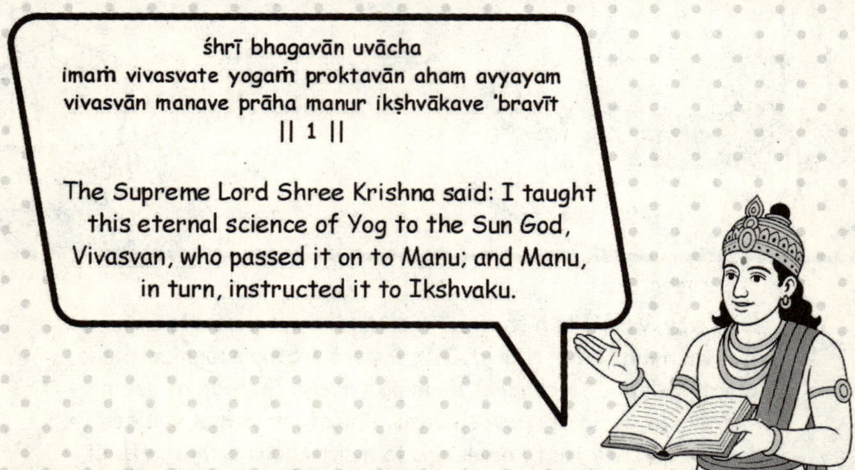
śhrī bhagavān uvācha
imaṁ vivasvate yogaṁ proktavān aham avyayam
vivasvān manave prāha manur ikṣhvākave 'bravīt
|| 1 ||
The Supreme Lord Shree Krishna said: I taught this eternal science of Yog to the Sun God, Vivasvan, who passed it on to Manu; and Manu, in turn, instructed it to Ikshvaku.

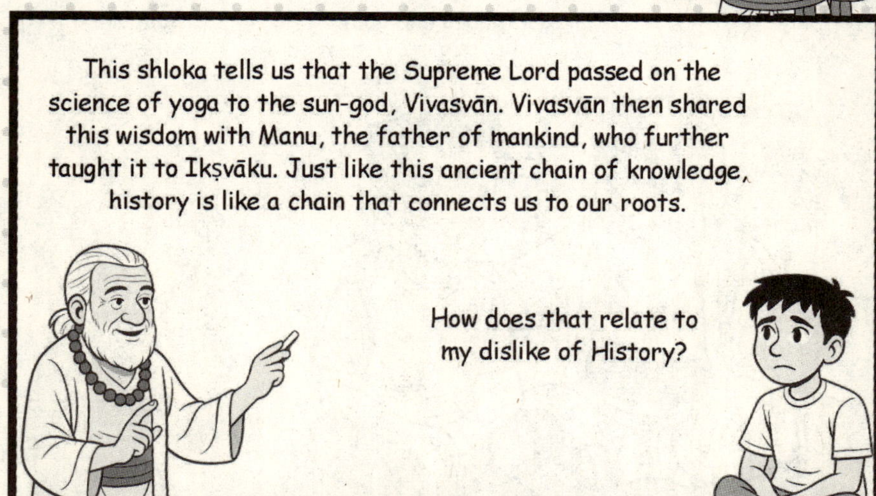
This shloka tells us that the Supreme Lord passed on the science of yoga to the sun-god, Vivasvān. Vivasvān then shared this wisdom with Manu, the father of mankind, who further taught it to Ikṣvāku. Just like this ancient chain of knowledge, history is like a chain that connects us to our roots.
How does that relate to my dislike of History?

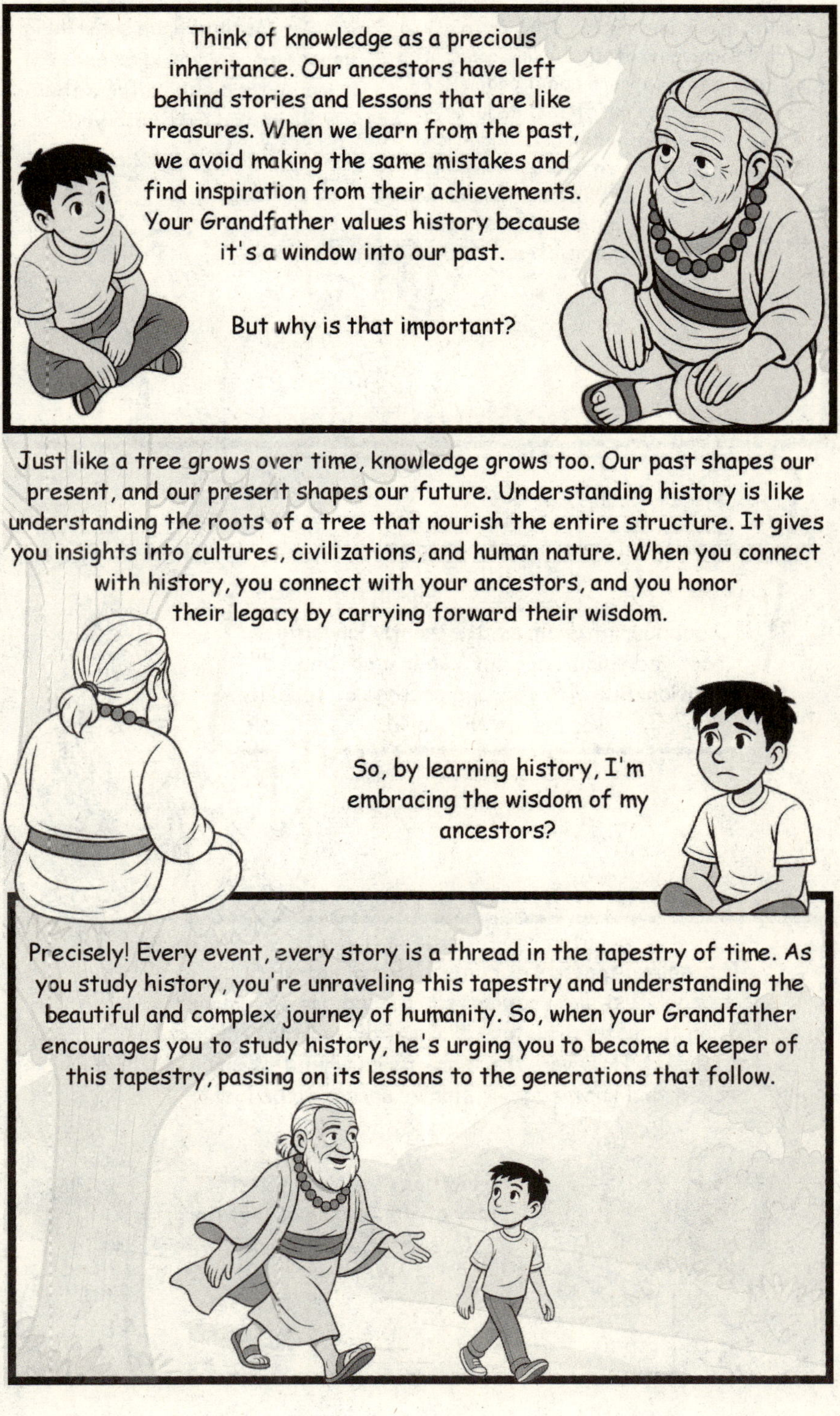
Think of knowledge as a precious inheritance. Our ancestors have left behind stories and lessons that are like treasures. When we learn from the past, we avoid making the same mistakes and find inspiration from their achievements. Your Grandfather values history because it's a window into our past.
But why is that important?
Just like a tree grows over time, knowledge grows too. Our past shapes our present, and our present shapes our future. Understanding history is like understanding the roots of a tree that nourish the entire structure. It gives you insights into cultures, civilizations, and human nature. When you connect with history, you connect with your ancestors, and you honor their legacy by carrying forward their wisdom.
So, by learning history, I'm embracing the wisdom of my ancestors?
Precisely! Every event, every story is a thread in the tapestry of time. As you study history, you're unraveling this tapestry and understanding the beautiful and complex journey of humanity. So, when your Grandfather encourages you to study history, he's urging you to become a keeper of this tapestry, passing on its lessons to the generations that follow.

Guruji, in our history class, we were asked to find something about Julius Caesar. It's so interesting to learn about people from the past. I found out that the Library of Alexandria — one of the most significant libraries of the ancient world — was burnt by the fire he lit. It made me wonder how many other fascinating stories might be lost or forgotten.
You've touched upon something important, my young friend. Let me share a shloka from the Bhagavad Gita with you.
evaṁ paramparā-prāptam imaṁ rājarṣhayo viduḥ
sa kāleneha mahatā yogo naṣhṭaḥ parantapa
|| 2 ||
O subduer of enemies, the saintly kings thus received this science of Yog in a continuous tradition. But with the long passage of time, it was lost to the world.
This shloka teaches us about the chain of disciplic succession. Just like knowledge is passed down from one generation to another, history is also a thread that connects us to the past. However, there are times when this chain is broken, and knowledge or stories appear to be lost.
How does that apply to the story of Julius Caesar and the Library of Alexandria?

The Library of Alexandria, with its vast collection of scrolls and knowledge, was a symbol of the past's brilliance. Yet, it was lost due to various reasons. Similarly, there might be many stories in history that are lesser-known or forgotten over time. But just because a story isn't widely known doesn't mean it's any less significant. Exploring lesser-known aspects of history can reveal remarkable stories of human achievements and struggles.
So, by learning more about history, I can uncover hidden gems of stories?
Exactly! When you approach history with curiosity, you're like an explorer unearthing tales from the past. These stories can inspire you, teaching you about human resilience, creativity, and the lessons of the past.
That's really interesting, Guruji. I want to explore more hidden stories now.

Guruji, today during our History test, I saw many of my classmates cheating. I know cheating is wrong, but I wasn't sure what to do about it. I kept wondering that god will punish them and the teacher will catch them cheating. But now I wonder if God even exists, because no one got caught!
It's natural to feel conflicted in situations like these. Let me share a shloka from the Bhagavad Gita that might offer some guidance.
yadā yadā hi dharmasya glānir bhavati bhārata abhyutthānam adharmasya tadātmānaṁ sṛijāmyaham || 7 ||
Whenever there is a decline in righteousness and an increase in unrighteousness, O Arjun, at that time I manifest Myself on earth.

Just like in times when darkness overshadows the light, a higher force intervenes to bring back harmony. So, have faith that goodness will prevail, even in challenging situations.
But it's just frustrating to see dishonesty being rewarded.
I understand your frustration, my child. Sometimes, it might seem like wrongdoings go unnoticed, and that can shake our faith. While we may not always witness immediate consequences, remember that the universal order has its ways of restoring fairness.
So, you're saying that even if my classmates got away with cheating this time, there might be consequences later?
It's possible, my child. And even if we don't see those consequences directly, it's important to remember that our actions, both good and bad, shape our character and the world around us. By choosing to do the right thing, you're contributing to a better future, regardless of immediate outcomes.
Thank you, Guruji. Your words give me hope that goodness will prevail, even when things seem unfair.

Guruji, I participated in the Western Culture and Society Quiz, but my team lost, and I got so many answers wrong. I thought I had prepared well. I thought I was starting to like History, but now I'm not so sure.
It's alright to feel frustrated when things don't go the way we expect. Let me share a shloka with you.

vīta-rāga-bhaya-krodhā man-mayā mām upāśhritāḥ
bahavo jñāna-tapasā pūtā mad-bhāvam āgatāḥ
|| 10 ||
Being free from attachment, fear, and anger, becoming fully absorbed in Me, and taking refuge in Me, many persons in the past became purified by knowledge of Me, and thus attained My divine love.

The shloka teaches the idea of letting go of negative emotions and attachments, seeking a higher perspective, and walking on the path of self-improvement and inner growth. Remember, it's not just about memorizing dates and events, but about understanding the journey of human civilization.
But I wanted to do well in the quiz, Guruji.
I know you did, and it's great that you put in effort. However, sometimes outcomes don't reflect our efforts accurately. Instead of feeling frustrated, reflect on the knowledge you gained during your preparation. What topics intrigued you the most?
But I'm still upset about losing.
Losing is a part of life, my child. It's important to let go of attachment to results, fear of not performing well, and anger upon failure. These emotions can hinder your joy of learning. Instead, focus on the goal, on gaining a deeper understanding of history. By doing so, you will purify your learning experience and discover a genuine love for the subject.
I now understand, Guruji. It's not just about the quiz; it's about my journey of discovering and appreciating history.

Guruji, today in History class, we learned about the four categories of occupations created based on qualities and duties. But I'm a bit confused about who actually created this system.
Ah, you're talking about the fourfold division of occupations - Brahmins, Kshatriyas, Vaishyas, and Shudras. It's an interesting concept. In the Bhagavad Gita, Lord Krishna explains that He is the creator of this system according to people's qualities and actions.
chātur-varṇyaṁ mayā sṛiṣhṭaṁ guṇa-karma-vibhāgaśhaḥ
tasya kartāram api māṁ viddhyakartāram avyayam
|| 13||
The four categories of occupations were created by Me according to people's qualities and activities. Although I am the Creator of this system, know Me to be the Non-doer and Eternal.
Wait, you mean Lord Krishna Himself created this system?
Yes, that's right. He established these categories to ensure a balanced and functional society where each person contributes according to their strengths and responsibilities. But even though He created the system, Lord Krishna describes Himself as the non-doer and eternal. He set this system in motion, but remains beyond the dualities of action and inaction.

I'm not sure I understand. How can He be both the creator and non-doer?
Imagine you're playing a game. You create the rules and structure, but once the game starts, you're no longer directly controlling every move. Similarly, the divine presence established this system to guide society, but it doesn't mean He is constantly intervening in every action.

So, He's like a silent observer?
Yes, in a way. He allows the natural flow of actions to take place while remaining untouched by them. Just as you fulfill your responsibilities at school, the divine's creation of this system is part of fulfilling its role in the grand scheme of things.

Guruji, I've been doing well in History, but I'm worried that next year the subject might become more difficult, and I won't be able to cope with it again.
It's natural to have concerns, my child. But let me share a shloka with you that might provide some guidance.
tad viddhi praṇipātena paripraśhnena sevayā
upadekṣhyanti te jñānaṁ jñāninas tattva-darśhinaḥ
|| 34 ||
Learn the Truth by approaching a spiritual master. Inquire from him with reverence and render service unto him. Such an enlightened Saint can impart knowledge unto you because he has seen the Truth.
This shloka emphasizes three important steps for seeking knowledge. The first step is 'praṇipātena,' which means approaching your teachers with humility and respect. When you approach your teachers with an open mind and show respect for their knowledge, it creates a positive environment for learning.
That makes sense. What's the second step?

The second step is 'paripraśnena,' which means asking meaningful and thoughtful questions. Don't hesitate to inquire deeply about the subjects that interest you. Questioning helps you gain clarity and a deeper understanding.
I see. And the third step?
The third step is 'sevayā,' which means rendering service to your teachers. Show your gratitude and willingness to learn by respectfully serving your teachers. This builds a strong teacher-student relationship and enhances your learning experience.
So, by following these steps, I can improve my learning experience?
Absolutely. When you approach learning with humility and, curiosity, you create an environment where knowledge can flow from your teachers to you. Remember that seeking knowledge is a noble pursuit, and the guidance of experienced mentors can provide you with valuable insights and understanding.
Thank you, Guruji. I feel more confident about approaching my studies now.

Adhyaya 5
Guruji, I won the qualifier tournament, but I don't feel as happy as I thought I would. I was up against Ethan, a boy from a different school. He didn't have proper equipment, training facilities, you name it; lesser privilege in every aspect.
Ah, my dear child, it's commendable that you are reflecting on this. Let me share a shloka from the Bhagavad Gita that might offer some guidance.
vidyā-vinaya-sampanne brāhmaṇe gavi hastini
śhuni chaiva śhva-pāke cha paṇḍitāḥ sama-darśhinaḥ
|| 18 ||
The truly learned, with the eyes of divine knowledge, see with equal vision a Brahmin, a cow, an elephant, a dog, and a dog-eater.
This shloka teaches us about seeing all living beings with equal vision. A true sage looks beyond external differences and treats everyone with respect and empathy. Just as a learned and gentle brāhmaṇa deserves respect, so does a cow, an elephant, a dog, and even a dog-eater. The essence of this teaching is to recognize the inherent value of every living being.
So, you mean I should have treated my opponent with more empathy and respect, regardless of his skill level?

Exactly, my child. It's not about the level of skill or resources someone has. It's about acknowledging their efforts, courage, and determination. Your opponent displayed tremendous courage by participating, even with limited resources. By appreciating his efforts, you uplift his spirit and promote the values of compassion and sportsmanship.
I understand now, Guruji. Winning is important, but treating everyone with fairness, respect, and empathy matters even more.

You've grasped the essence of the teaching, my young champion. Remember, a truly noble heart recognizes the worth of all beings and treats them with kindness and compassion. Your victory is meaningful when it's accompanied by these virtues.
Thank you, Guruji. I'll keep this in mind not just in sports but in all aspects of life.
BHAGAVAD GITA

Guruji, I'm really excited! I've made it to the final tournament of table tennis, and my father promised to buy me my favourite sneakers if I win. I really want those sneakers, and I want to win, no matter what.
It's wonderful to see your enthusiasm and determination, my young friend. Winning a tournament is indeed a commendable goal. However, let me share a shloka from the Bhagavad Gita that might offer you some valuable insights.
ye hi sansparśha-jā bhogā duḥkha-yonaya eva te
ādyantavantaḥ kaunteya na teṣhu ramate budhaḥ
|| 22 ||
The pleasures that arise from contact with the sense objects, though appearing as enjoyable to worldly-minded people, are verily a source of misery. O son of Kunti, such pleasures have a beginning and an end, so the wise do not delight in them.

This shloka teaches us about the fleeting nature of material pleasures. It suggests that such pleasures are sources of misery because they are temporary and come to an end. Wise individuals don't derive lasting happiness from these external pleasures.
So, are you saying I shouldn't want those sneakers or aim to win the tournament?
No, not at all. It's natural to desire things and set goals. What's important is not becoming overly attached to the outcomes. Just remember, winning the tournament is a great achievement, but such happiness is temporary. Instead of focusing solely on the outcome, focus on playing with joy, embracing the challenges, and giving your best. This way, you'll find satisfaction in the journey itself, regardless of the end result.
So, I should enjoy the game and not let the desire for the sneakers control me?
Exactly. Enjoy the game, relish the competition, and play with your heart. Don't let the attachment to the sneakers steal your joy. By doing so, you'll not only excel in the sport but also cultivate a mindset that brings you lasting happiness, irrespective of external achievements..

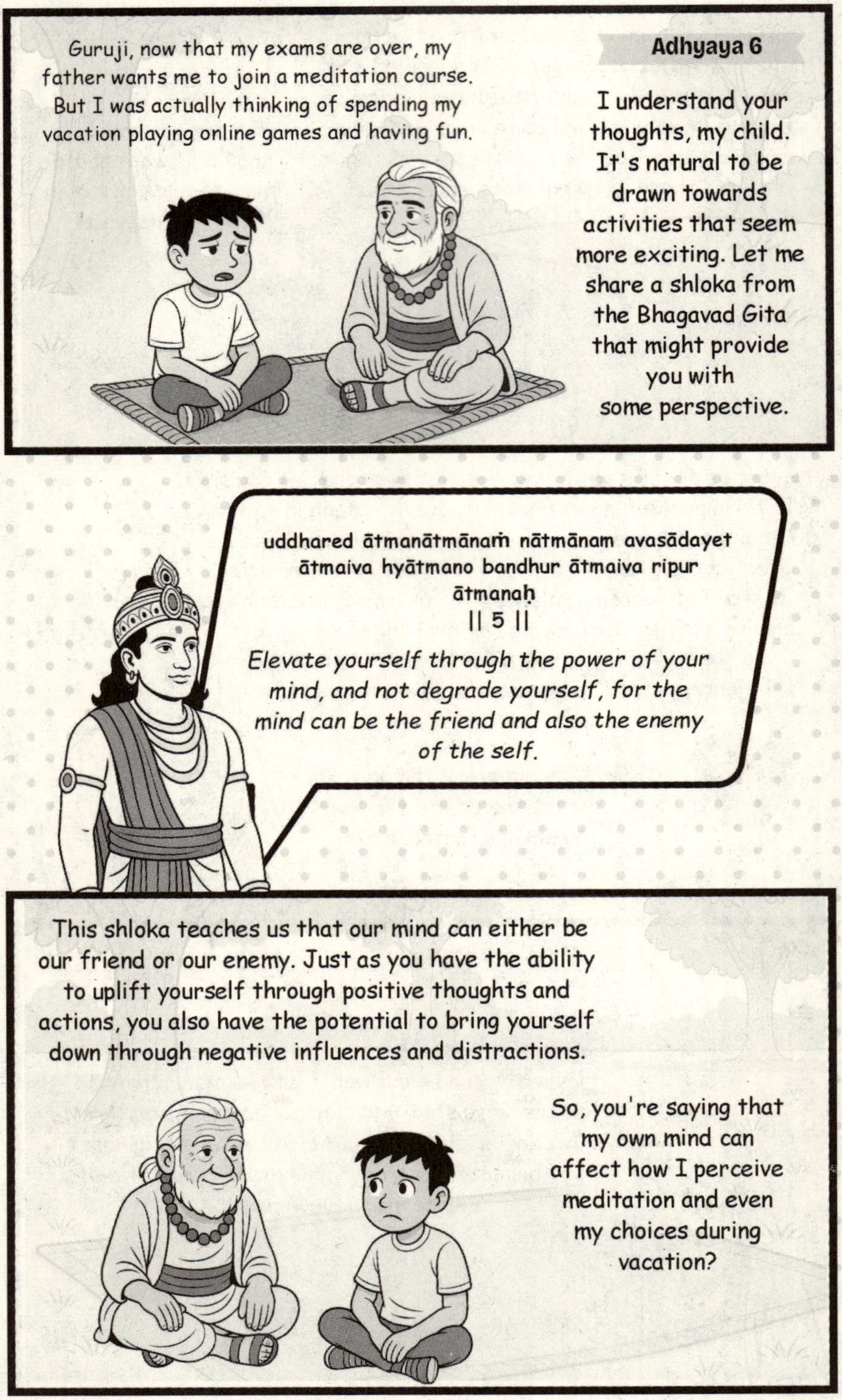
Guruji, now that my exams are over, my father wants me to join a meditation course. But I was actually thinking of spending my vacation playing online games and having fun.
Adhyaya 6
I understand your thoughts, my child. It's natural to be drawn towards activities that seem more exciting. Let me share a shloka from the Bhagavad Gita that might provide you with some perspective.
uddhared ātmanātmānaṁ nātmānam avasādayet
ātmaiva hyātmano bandhur ātmaiva ripur
ātmanaḥ
|| 5 ||
Elevate yourself through the power of your mind, and not degrade yourself, for the mind can be the friend and also the enemy of the self.
This shloka teaches us that our mind can either be our friend or our enemy. Just as you have the ability to uplift yourself through positive thoughts and actions, you also have the potential to bring yourself down through negative influences and distractions.
So, you're saying that my own mind can affect how I perceive meditation and even my choices during vacation?

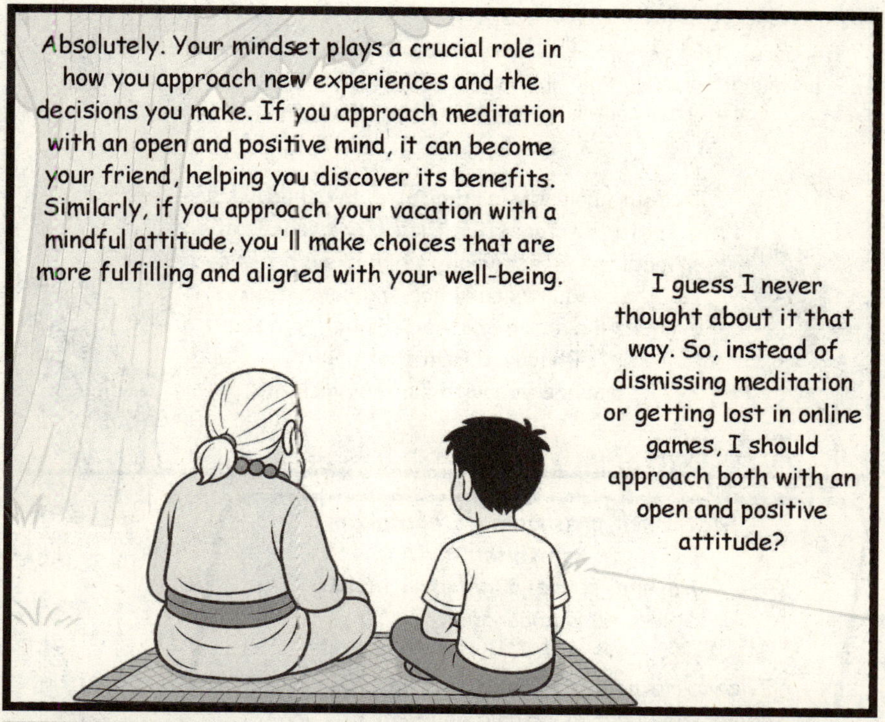
Absolutely. Your mindset plays a crucial role in how you approach new experiences and the decisions you make. If you approach meditation with an open and positive mind, it can become your friend, helping you discover its benefits. Similarly, if you approach your vacation with a mindful attitude, you'll make choices that are more fulfilling and aligred with your well-being.
I guess I never thought about it that way. So, instead of dismissing meditation or getting lost in online games, I should approach both with an open and positive attitude?

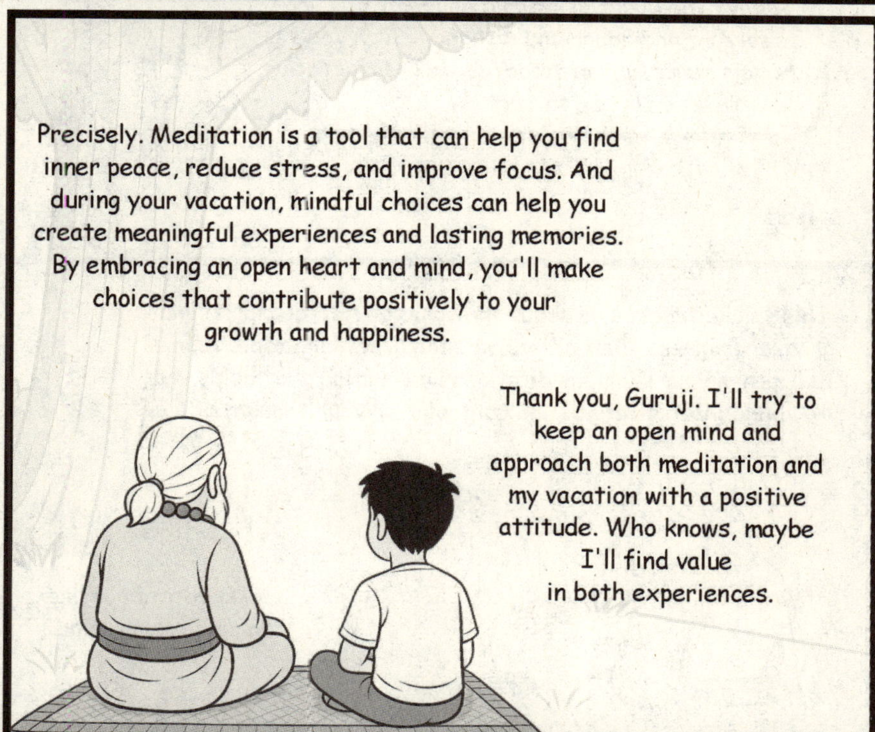
Precisely. Meditation is a tool that can help you find inner peace, reduce stress, and improve focus. And during your vacation, mindful choices can help you create meaningful experiences and lasting memories. By embracing an open heart and mind, you'll make choices that contribute positively to your growth and happiness.
Thank you, Guruji. I'll try to keep an open mind and approach both meditation and my vacation with a positive attitude. Who knows, maybe I'll find value in both experiences.

Guruji, I've been thinking more about meditation and how it can really make a difference in my life. But I still have some doubts. How can sitting quietly and controlling my mind bring about any real benefits?
Your curiosity is admirable, my child. It's natural to question the effectiveness of meditation, especially when it's a practice that requires patience and consistency. Let me share another shloka from the Bhagavad Gita that might provide you with further insights.
jitātmanaḥ praśhāntasya paramātmā samāhitaḥ
śhītoṣhṇa-sukha-duḥkheṣhu tathā mānāpamānayoḥ
|| 7 ||
The yogis who have conquered the mind rise above the dualities of cold and heat, joy and sorrow, and honor and dishonor. Such yogis remain peaceful and steadfast in their devotion to God.
This shloka teaches us about the value of self-discipline and gradual progress. Just as you've been practicing table tennis to improve your skills, meditation is a practice that helps you build inner strength and control over your thoughts.
So, meditation is like training for my mind?

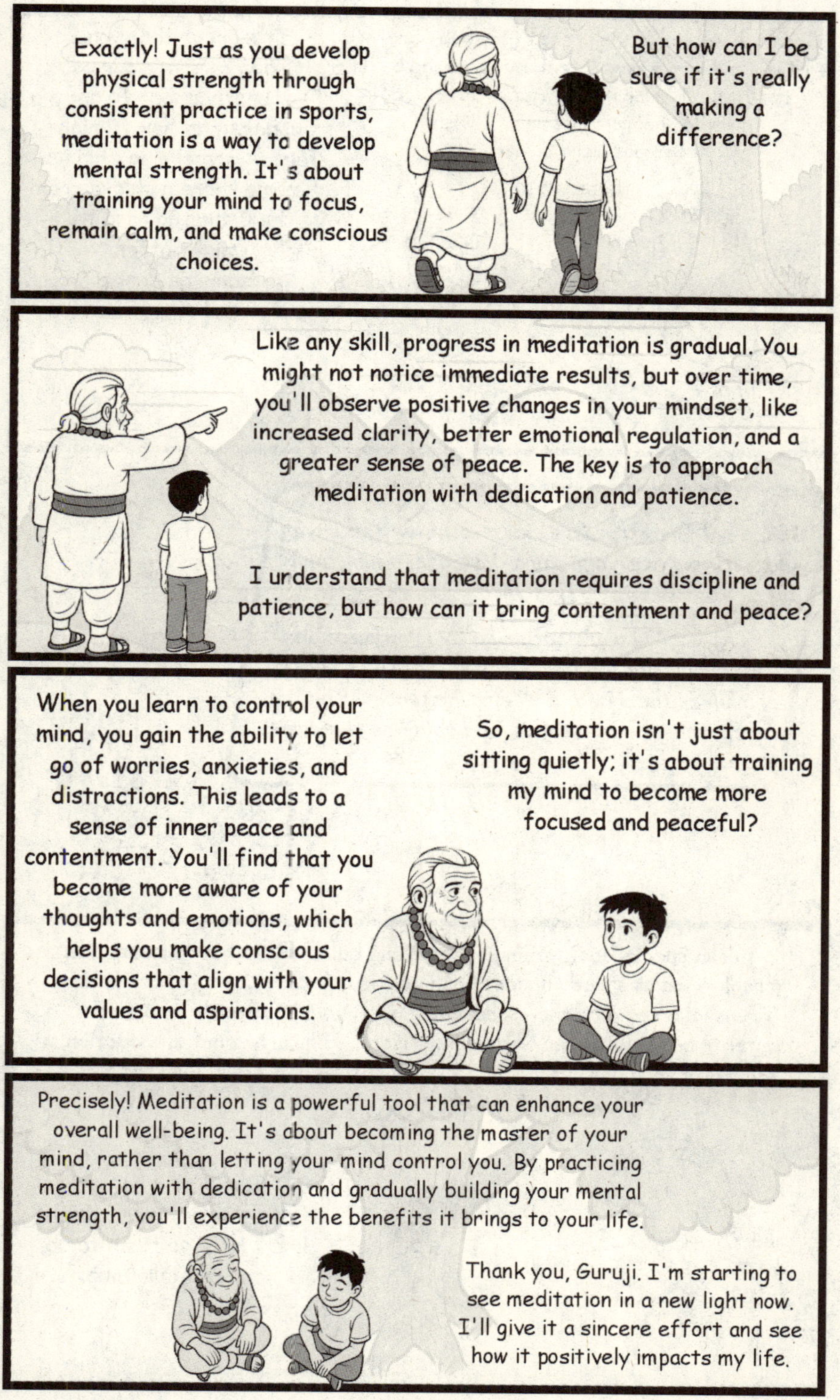

Exactly! Just as you develop physical strength through consistent practice in sports, meditation is a way to develop mental strength. It's about training your mind to focus, remain calm, and make conscious choices.
But how can I be sure if it's really making a difference?
Like any skill, progress in meditation is gradual. You might not notice immediate results, but over time, you'll observe positive changes in your mindset, like increased clarity, better emotional regulation, and a greater sense of peace. The key is to approach meditation with dedication and patience.
I understand that meditation requires discipline and patience, but how can it bring contentment and peace?
When you learn to control your mind, you gain the ability to let go of worries, anxieties, and distractions. This leads to a sense of inner peace and contentment. You'll find that you become more aware of your thoughts and emotions, which helps you make conscious decisions that align with your values and aspirations.
So, meditation isn't just about sitting quietly; it's about training my mind to become more focused and peaceful?
Precisely! Meditation is a powerful tool that can enhance your overall well-being. It's about becoming the master of your mind, rather than letting your mind control you. By practicing meditation with dedication and gradually building your mental strength, you'll experience the benefits it brings to your life.
Thank you, Guruji. I'm starting to see meditation in a new light now. I'll give it a sincere effort and see how it positively impacts my life.

Guruji, I've been taking care of my baby brother lately, and sometimes I feel overwhelmed by all the tasks. I know it's my responsibility, but there are moments when I wish things were easier.
It's great that you're taking care of your baby brother, but I can understand how it might feel overwhelming at times. Let me share a shloka from the Bhagavad Gita that might offer some guidance.

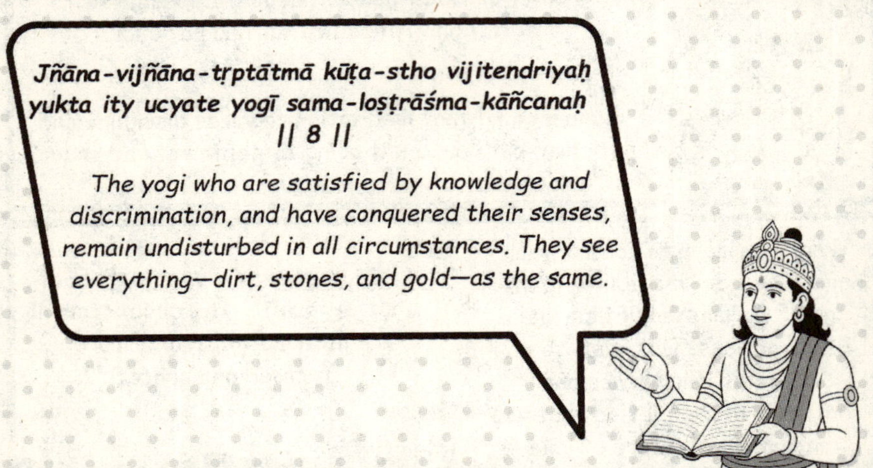
Jñāna-vijñāna-tṛptātmā kūṭa-stho vijitendriyaḥ
yukta ity ucyate yogī sama-loṣṭrāśma-kāñcanaḥ
|| 8 ||
The yogi who are satisfied by knowledge and discrimination, and have conquered their senses, remain undisturbed in all circumstances. They see everything—dirt, stones, and gold—as the same.

This shloka speaks about being content and balanced within yourself. Just as a rock remains steady amidst both gold and pebbles, you too can remain unshaken by external circumstances. A yogi is someone who finds contentment in both knowledge and wisdom. Similarly, find satisfaction in the tasks you perform, even if they might seem overwhelming at times.
But Guruji, it's not always easy. Sometimes I feel like I have so much to do, and so little time.

It's okay to have moments when focus wavers, but remember that a balanced mind is key. Like the yogi who remains unaffected by external circumstances, try to stay centered and composed. Even amidst challenges, your inner strength will guide you.
So, it's about finding balance and not letting tasks overwhelm me?

Exactly. By finding contentment within yourself, you'll be able to face challenges with a calm mind. Just as the shloka describes, a true yogi remains untouched by external situations and is anchored in their own centeredness.
I'll try my best to stay balanced and find satisfaction in my responsibilities.

Guruji, do you remember Ethan? Today, Raghav didn't treat Ethan well. He made fun of him, and it didn't feel
It's natural to feel troubled when we witness unkind behavior. Let me share a shloka from the Bhagavad Gita that might offer

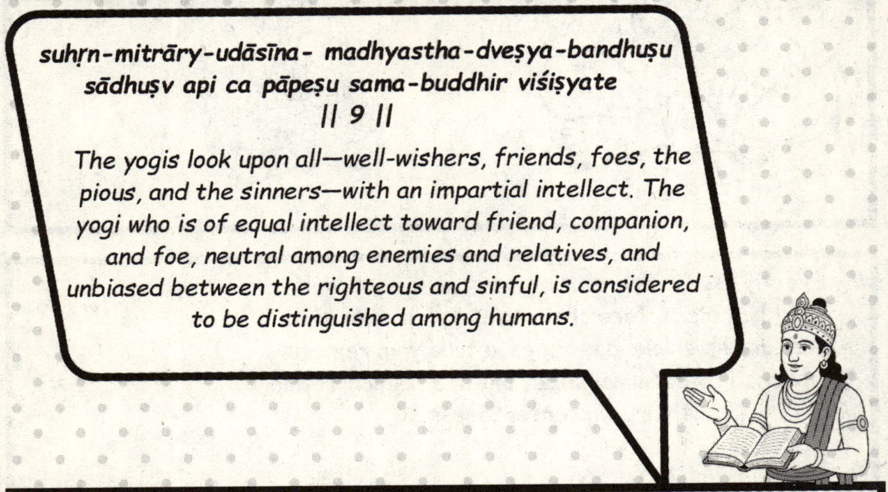
suhṛn-mitrāry-udāsīna- madhyastha-dveṣya-bandhuṣu
sādhuṣv api ca pāpeṣu sama-buddhir viśiṣyate
|| 9 ||
The yogis look upon all—well-wishers, friends, foes, the pious, and the sinners—with an impartial intellect. The yogi who is of equal intellect toward friend, companion, and foe, neutral among enemies and relatives, and unbiased between the righteous and sinful, is considered to be distinguished among humans.

This shloka speaks about having a balanced and impartial attitude towards everyone in various situations. Treating everyone fairly and equally, regardless of their status, helps us become better individuals.
So, it means we should treat everyone the same way, whether they are our friends, enemies, or strangers?

Yes, exactly. Just like the sun shines on everyone without discrimination, we too should treat others with love and respect, regardless of their background.
But what if someone is not kind to us? Should we still treat them the same way?

Absolutely. It's easy to be kind to those who are kind to us, but the shloka teaches us to rise above our personal feelings. By treating everyone equally, we set an example of compassion and understanding. By doing so, we gain respect, set a positive example, and contribute to a harmonious environment.
I think I understand now. I'll go to Raghav and tell him about this shloka!

Guruji, I attended a meditation camp and learned so many techniques, but I sometimes have trouble staying focused during my practice. My mind keeps wandering, and I can't seem to find the same calmness I felt during the camp.
It's completely normal to face challenges when starting a new practice, my child. Meditation requires patience and consistent effort. Let me share a shloka from the Bhagavad Gita that might offer some insights.
Yogī yuñjīta satatam ātmānaṁ rāhasya-sthitaḥ
ekākī yata-cittātma nirāśīr aparigrahaś
cākriyamāṇaḥ bhakta-mānaṁ sa me priyaḥ
|| 10 ||
Those who seek the state of Yog should reside in seclusion, constantly engaged in meditation with a controlled mind and body, getting rid of desires and possessions for enjoyment.

This shloka teaches us about the qualities of a true yogi, which are also essential for deepening your meditation practice. A yogi is someone who finds quiet moments for meditation, focuses on the inner world, and remains calm within.
But how do I do that, Guruji? My mind is always racing with thoughts.
The key lies in training your mind, my child. Just as an athlete practices to improve their skills, meditation requires consistent pract ce. Start by finding a peaceful and solitary place for your practice. Practice without attachment to the outcome. With dedication, you'll find that the qualities of a true yogi will naturally start blooming within you. That kind of meditation is not only successful but also dear to the greater power, the Divine.
Thank you, Guruji. I'll keep practicing and embodying the qualities of a yogi in my meditation journey.

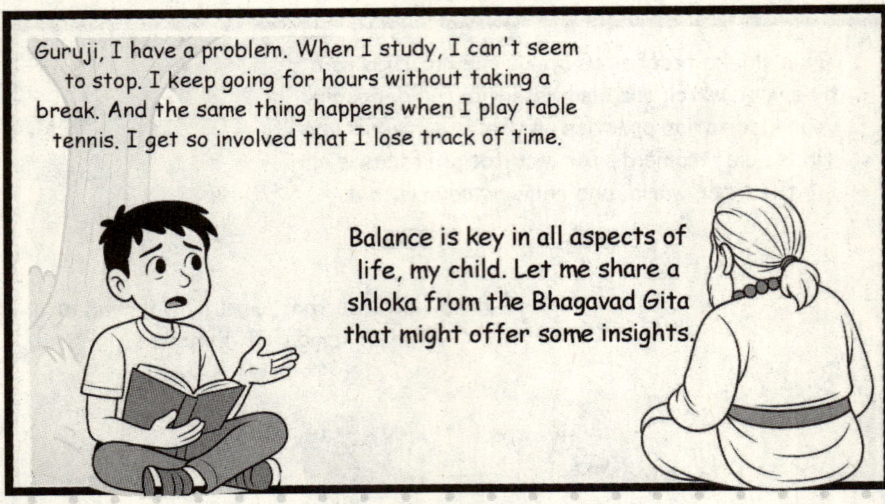
Guruji, I have a problem. When I study, I can't seem to stop. I keep going for hours without taking a break. And the same thing happens when I play table tennis. I get so involved that I lose track of time.
Balance is key in all aspects of life, my child. Let me share a shloka from the Bhagavad Gita that might offer some insights.

Nāty-aśnatastu yogo'sti na caikāntam-anaśnataḥ
na cāti-svapna-śīlasya jāgrato naiva cārjuna
|| 16 ||
O Arjun, those who eat too much or too little, sleep too much or too little, cannot attain success in Yog.

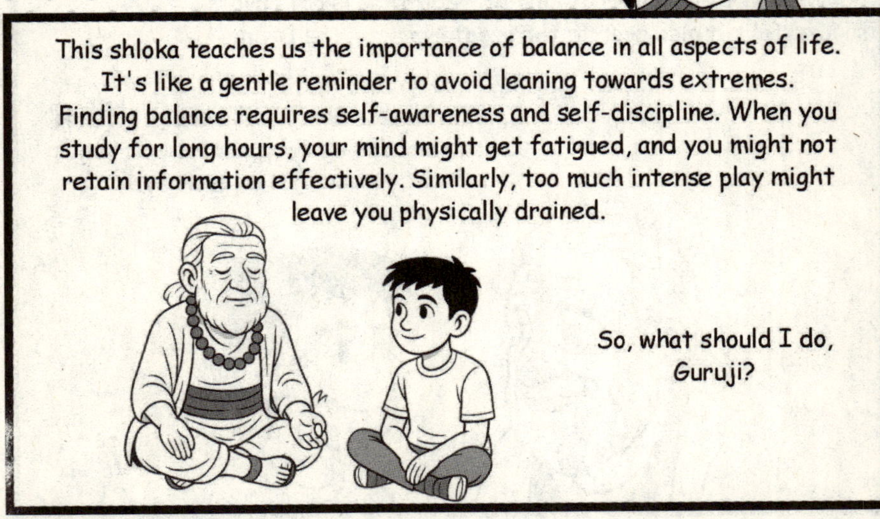
This shloka teaches us the importance of balance in all aspects of life. It's like a gentle reminder to avoid leaning towards extremes. Finding balance requires self-awareness and self-discipline. When you study for long hours, your mind might get fatigued, and you might not retain information effectively. Similarly, too much intense play might leave you physically drained.
So, what should I do, Guruji?

Moderation is the key. When you study, take short breaks in between. Stretch, take a walk, or just relax your mind. And during your playtime, set a time limit. When the time is up, step away from the game and engage in something else.
But I feel like I can't stop once I start!

That's where self-discipline comes into play, my child. Remember, balance and moderation lead to a more fulfilling and harmonious life journey. By practicing self-control, you're building a strong foundation for a healthier approach to both studying and playing.
Thank you, Guruji. I'll work on finding that balance and making self-discipline a part of my routine.

Adhyaya 7
Guruji, my mother seems really sad these days, especially with my aunt's recent passing. Todcy is her birthday, but she told us that she does not want to celebrate the day. It's making me question whether there's really a higher power or God. If there is, why would it allow such sadness to happen?
Let me share a perspective from the Bhagavad Gita that might offer some insight.

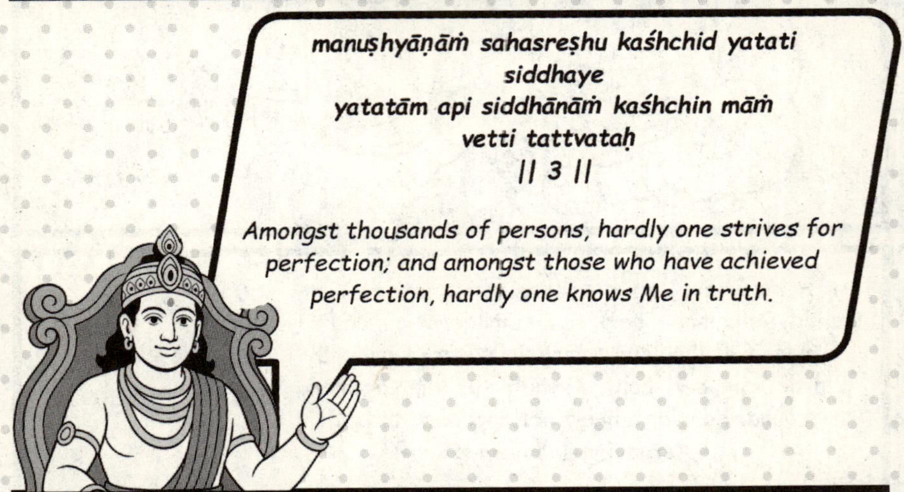
manuṣhyāṇāṁ sahasreṣhu kaśhchid yatati siddhaye
yatatām api siddhānāṁ kaśhchin māṁ vetti tattvataḥ
|| 3 ||
Amongst thousands of persons, hardly one strives for perfection; and amongst those who have achieved perfection, hardly one knows Me in truth.

This shloka reminds us that only a rare few individuals strive for spiritual enlightenment and deep understanding of the divine. Similarly, only a rare few grasp the true essence of God's existence and role in the grand tapestry of life.
So, you're saying that we might not fully understand God's plan or purpose in moments of sorrow?

Precisely. The workings of the universe are intricate and far-reaching. Faith doesn't eliminate suffering, but it can provide us with the strength and resilience to navigate through it. Our understanding of God's plan might be limited, but our capacity for compassion, empathy, and support for one another is boundless.
So, even when we don't have all the answers, our compassion and support can still make a difference?
Absolutely, my child. Our ability to offer comfort to those who are suffering is a powerful way to bring light into the darkest of times. While we might not comprehend the entirety of God's plan, our capacity to create a positive impact in the lives of others is a reflection of the divine within us.

Guruji, I can't seem to shake off the feeling I had about the existence of a superior power.. Sometimes, it's hard to believe when there's so much suffering in the world. I mean, how can there be a divine presence in everything, especially when we witness so much pain?
Bhagavad Gita has a shloka just in this reference.
raso 'ham apsu kaunteya prabhasmi sasi-suryayoh
pranavah sarva-vedesu sabdah khe paurusam nrsu
|| 8 ||
I am the taste in water, O son of Kunti, and the radiance of the sun and the moon. I am the sacred syllable Om in the Vedic mantras; I am the sound in ether, and the ability in humans.
Think about water - its taste, essential for life, is a reflection of the divine essence. Similarly, the light of the moon and the sun, vital for our world, is a glimpse of the divine's radiance.
But, Guruji, I've learned about 'Om' in the Vedas. How does that fit in?

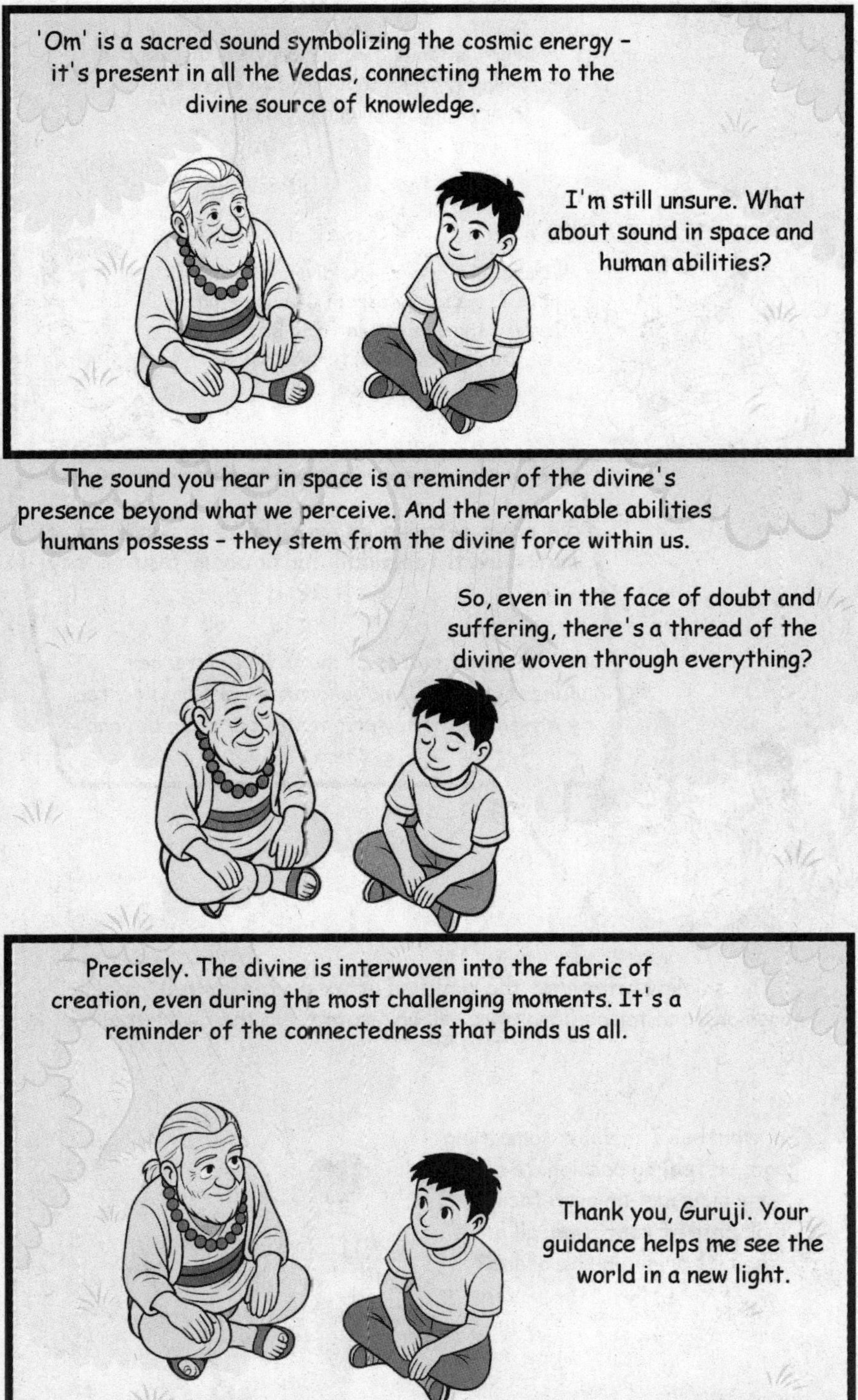
'Om' is a sacred sound symbolizing the cosmic energy - it's present in all the Vedas, connecting them to the divine source of knowledge.
I'm still unsure. What about sound in space and human abilities?
The sound you hear in space is a reminder of the divine's presence beyond what we perceive. And the remarkable abilities humans possess - they stem from the divine force within us.
So, even in the face of doubt and suffering, there's a thread of the divine woven through everything?
Precisely. The divine is interwoven into the fabric of creation, even during the most challenging moments. It's a reminder of the connectedness that binds us all.
Thank you, Guruji. Your guidance helps me see the world in a new light.

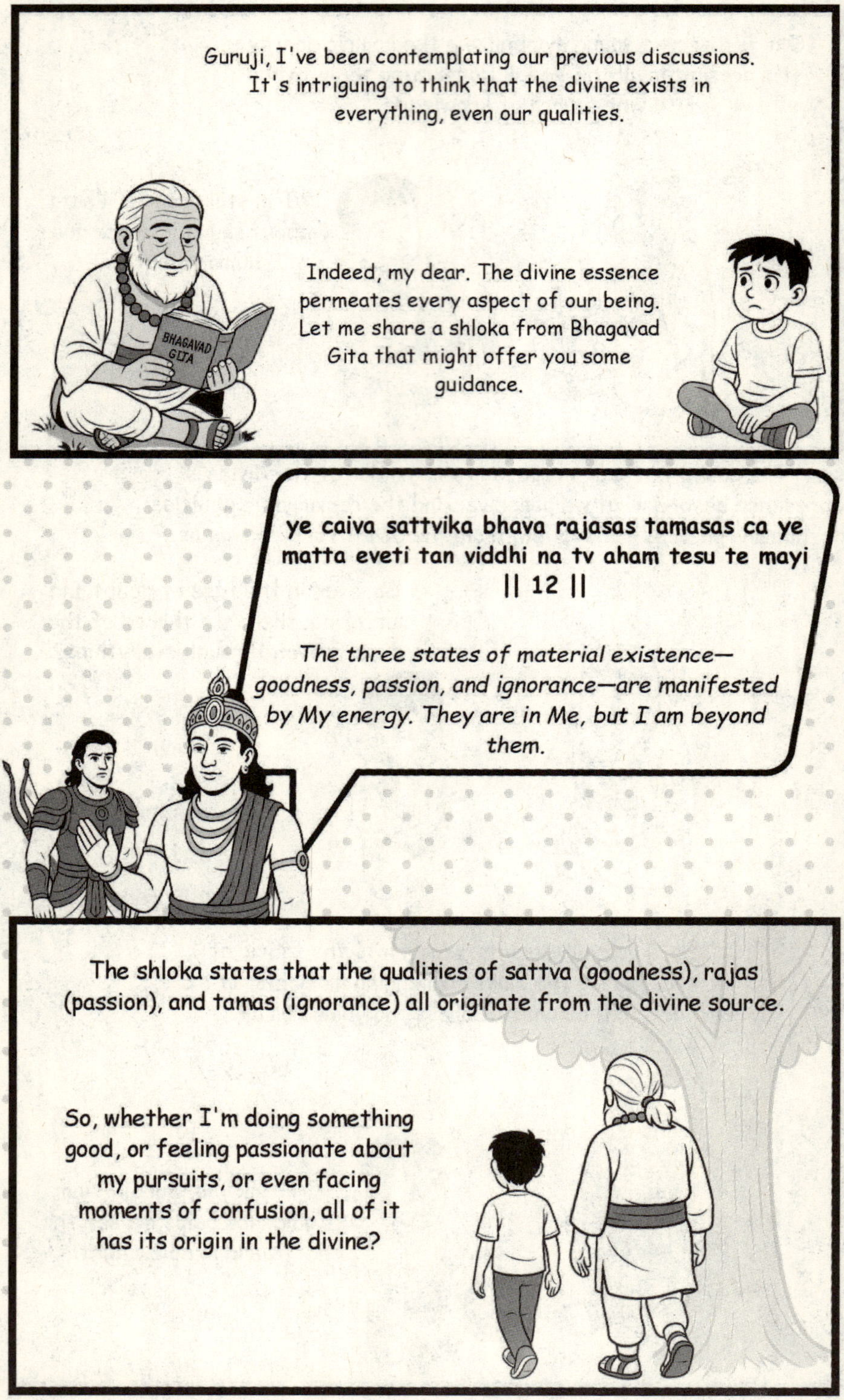
Guruji, I've been contemplating our previous discussions. It's intriguing to think that the divine exists in everything, even our qualities.
Indeed, my dear. The divine essence permeates every aspect of our being. Let me share a shloka from Bhagavad Gita that might offer you some guidance.
BHAGAVAD GITA
ye caiva sattvika bhava rajasas tamasas ca ye matta eveti tan viddhi na tv aham tesu te mayi || 12 ||
The three states of material existence—goodness, passion, and ignorance—are manifested by My energy. They are in Me, but I am beyond them.
The shloka states that the qualities of sattva (goodness), rajas (passion), and tamas (ignorance) all originate from the divine source.
So, whether I'm doing something good, or feeling passionate about my pursuits, or even facing moments of confusion, all of it has its origin in the divine?

Precisely. The qualities of sattva, rajas, and tamas are like threads woven into the fabric of existence, each serving a purpose in our growth.
But Guruji, does that mean the divine is equally present in both my moments of kindness and my moments of confusion?

The divine exists as the foundation of these qualities, yet it's essential to understand that the qualities themselves are within the divine, not the other way around. The qualities spring from the divine source, but they do not define the divine. They are opportunities for us to make choices and evolve.
Thank you, Guruji. Your wisdom guides me to look at life with a broader perspective.

Guruji, I've been wondering about those who don't believe in God or the divine. What happens to them?
It's a profound question you're asking, my dear. Here's what Bhagavad Gita has to say in this regard:
na mam duskrtino mudhah prapadyante naradhamah
mayayapahrta-jnana asuram bhavam asritah
|| 15 ||
Four kinds of people do not surrender unto Me—those ignorant of knowledge, those who lazily follow their lower nature though capable of knowing Me, those with deluded intellect, and those with a demoniac nature.

According to the shloka, those who don't recognize the divine or are led astray by illusion and ignorance may not surrender to the divine's presence. The divine's presence is always around us, but some may be swayed by illusion or ignorance, clouding their understanding.
So, it's not that they're bad people necessarily?

Correct. The shloka emphasizes that those who are misguided by illusion or ignorance might not see the divine's presence. It doesn't label them as bad people, but rather as individuals whose understanding has been veiled. The divine's presence is open to all who seek it. By exploring their own experiences, learning, and seeking knowledge, individuals can overcome the barriers of illusion and ignorance and find their own path to understanding the divine.
That's reassuring, Guruji. It's important to remember that people might have different journeys in their understanding of the divine.

Guruji, how would I know if I'm praying to God correctly?
A thoughtful question, my dear. Let me share with you a shloka from the Bhagavad Gita that might shed some light on this.
udarah sarva evaite jnani tv atmaiva me matam asthitah sa hi yuktatma mam evanuttamam gatim || 18 ||
All those who are devoted to Me are indeed noble. But those in knowledge, who are of steadfast mind, whose intellect is merged in Me, and who have made Me alone as their supreme goal, I consider as My very self.
The shloka tells us that all individuals who possess nobility, wisdom, and devotion are dear to the divine. But the one who is not only virtuous but also steadfastly united with the divine within themselves, that person is considered to have reached the ultimate destination.
So, it's not just about reciting prayers?

Exactly. my child. While reciting prayers is one way to connect with the divine, what truly matters is the sincerity and devotion you put into it. It's about cultivating virtues like kindness, compassion, and self - awareness in your daily life.
How can I become steadfastly united with the divine?
By recognizing the divine presence within yourself and others, and by living a life that aligns with virtues and values. When you treat others with love, when you seek wisdom and grow spiritually, and when you see the interconnectedness of all beings, you are on the right path.
Thank you Guruji! I'll remember this.

Guruji, I believe in the divine power, but sometimes I can't go to the temple along with my parents when I have to study. Is that a bad thing on my part?
Not at all, my child. The divine understands the commitments and responsibilities we have in our lives, including our studies.

But Guruji, my parents say that going to the temple is important, and I feel torn between my studies and my devotion.
It's wonderful that you value both your studies and your devotion. The divine's presence is not limited to a physical place. Your sincere belief and heartfelt devotion matter more than the location.

So, can I pray and connect with the divine even when I can't go to the temple?
Absolutely. Here's a shloka from Bhagavad Gita that will help you understand the situation better.

yo yo yam yam tanum bhaktah
sraddhayarcitum icchati
tasya tasyacalam sraddham tam eva
vidadhamy aham
|| 21 ||
Whatever celestial form a devotee seeks to worship with faith, I steady the faith of such a devotee in that form.
The shloka teaches us that whatever form a devotee with faith wishes to worship, the civine makes that faith steady. Your devotion is what matters, and you can connect with the divine through prayer and contemplation, even from your study space.
Thank you, Guruji. I was worried that I might be disappointing the divine by not going to the temple.
Remember, my child, the divine's understanding is vast and compassionate. Your sincerity and devotion shine through your actions, whether you're in a temple or at home studying. Your heartfelt connection matters the most.

Guruji, if I pray to the god, will the god fulfill all my wishes?
That's an interesting question, my child. Let me tell you a shloka from Bhagavad Gita.
BHAGAVAD GITA
antavat tu phalam tesam tad bhavaty alpa-medhasam
devan deva-yajo yanti mad-bhakta yanti mam api
|| 23 ||
But the fruit gained by these people of little understanding is perishable. Those who worship the celestial gods go to the celestial abodes, while My devotees come to Me.
The shloka explains that those with limited intelligence seek transient results, often driven by their desires. It's like aiming for things that provide temporary satisfaction but may not lead to lasting fulfillment.
So, does that mean praying to god won't fulfill my wishes?

It means that while praying to the divine, it's good to ask for guidance, strength, and wisdom rather than just material gains. The real fulfillment comes from aligning your desires with higher values and seeking a deeper connection with the divine.
So, it's more about the kind of wishes I have?
Exactly, my child. Praying for qualities like love, kindness, and wisdom will bring lasting joy. The divine will guide you towards what truly matters for your growth and happiness.

Guruji, today when I was praying to god, my father told me that if I am a true devotee, god will present himself to me. Is it true that god can present himself and take a human form?
Ah, an interesting question, my child. Let me share a shloka from the Bhagavad Gita that might help clarify this.
avyaktam vyaktim apannam manyante mam abuddhayah
param bhavam ajananto mamavyayam anuttamam
|| 24 ||
The less intelligent think that I, the Supreme Lord Shree Krishna, was formless earlier and have now assumed this personality. They do not understand the imperishable exalted nature of My personal form.

The shloka tells us that unintelligent people might think of the divine as having taken a human form. However, they don't fully understand the higher, eternal, and supreme nature of the divine.
So, does that mean god cannot take a human form?
It's not about what god can or cannot do, but rather about our understanding and perception. The divine is beyond human comprehension, and while some may believe in manifestations of the divine in human form, it's important to also explore the higher truths and eternal nature of the divine. Spirituality is a journey of seeking higher truths and connecting with the divine in ways that resonate with your heart and soul. Keep an open mind and explore the vastness of spirituality.
Thank you, Guruji. This helps me a lot.

Adhyaya 8
Guruji, we had gone to aunt's house today for her death anniversary. During the pooja today, I couldn't help but think about what happens after someone passes away. Is there a way we can be sure that they are at peace?
Those are deep questions, my child, and they're a natural part of our curiosity about life and its mysteries. Let me share a shloka from the Bhagavad Gita that might help shed some light on this.

anta-kāle ca mām eva smaran muktvā kalevaram
yaḥ prayāti sa mad-bhāvaṁ yāti nāsty atra saṁśayaḥ
|| 5 ||
Those who relinquish the body while remembering Me at the moment of death will come to Me. There is certainly no doubt about this.

The shloka tells us that whoever departs from this life while remembering the divine, they surely attain the divine nature. It teaches us about the power of remembrance during important life moments, like the end of life. By focusing on the divine and letting go of the physical body, one can find a sense of peace and connection with the greater reality.
So, you mean that by thinking of the divine, we can ensure a peaceful journey even after death?

Yes, my child. It's about approaching life's transitions with a sense of faith and connection to the divine. By focusing on the spiritual aspect, we can find solace and reassurance that there's something beyond the physical realm.
Thank you, Guruji. That brings some comfort to my thoughts.

Guruji, ever since we've come back from aunt's death anniversary pooja, my mother has been feeling sad. I want to help her feel better, but I don't know how.
It's truly compassionate of you to want to comfort your mother during this time, my dear. Let me share a shloka from the Bhagavad Gita that might provide you with some guidance.

tasmāt sarveṣu kāleṣu mām anusmara yudhya ca
mayy arpita-mano-buddhir mām evaiṣyasy asaṁśayaḥ
|| 7 ||
Therefore, always remember Me and also do your duty of fighting the war. With mind and intellect surrendered to Me, you will definitely attain Me; of this, there is no doubt.

The shloka advises us to remember the divine at all times and to continue our efforts, even in challenging moments. It teaches us that by surrendering our mind and intellect to the divine, we can find the strength to face difficult situations.
So, you mean if we keep the divine in our thoughts and actions, we can find comfort and strength?
Exactly, my child. When we stay connected to the divine and keep our minds focused on spiritual values, it can bring us a sense of peace and provide us with the strength to support others, even in times of sadness.
Thank you, Guruji. I'll try my best to help my mother by sharing this with her.
That's a thoughtful gesture, my dear. Remember, by sharing these spiritual insights with your mother, you're offering her a way to find solace and strength during challenging times. Your compassion will surely make a positive impact on her feelings.

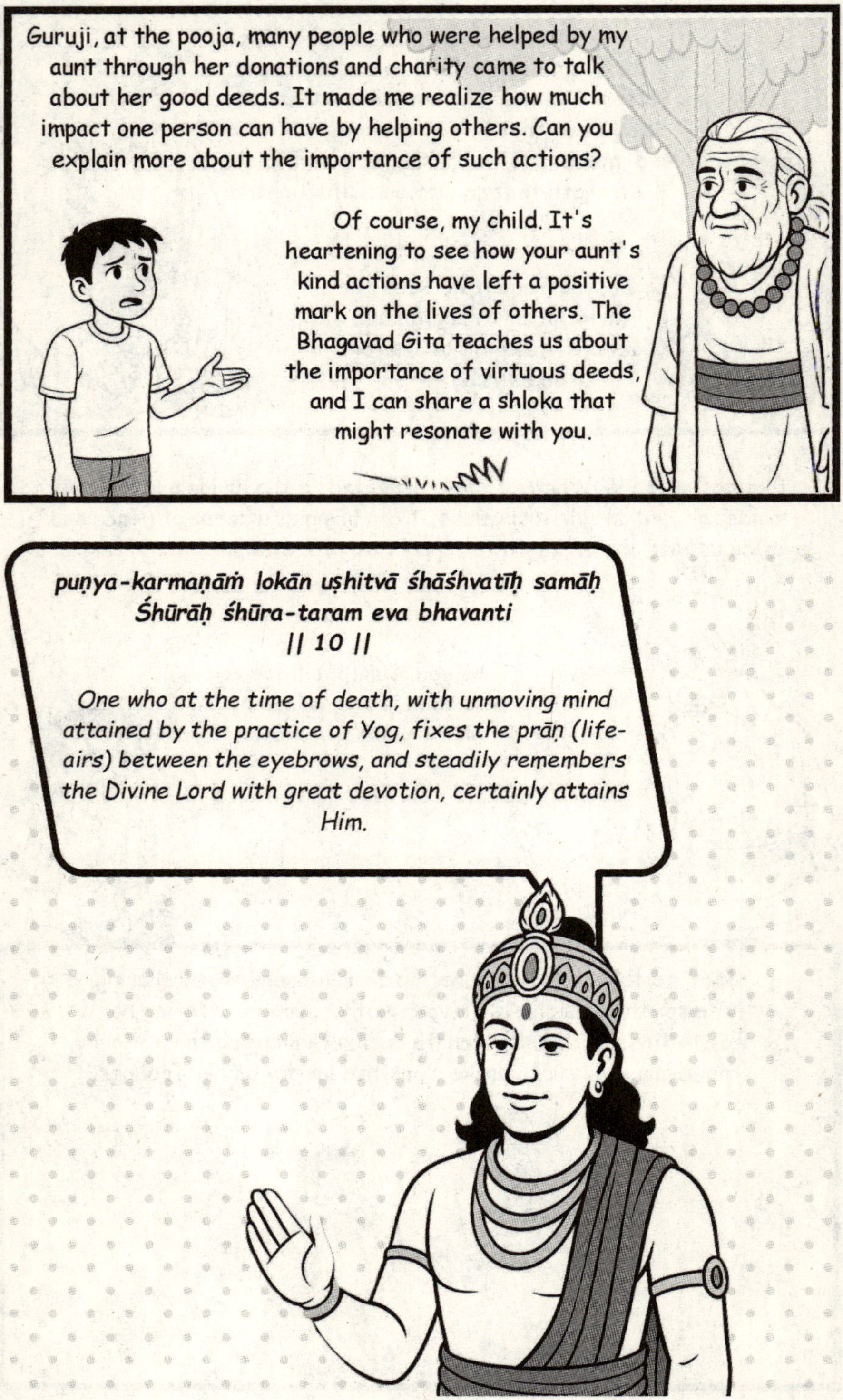
Guruji, at the pooja, many people who were helped by my aunt through her donations and charity came to talk about her good deeds. It made me realize how much impact one person can have by helping others. Can you explain more about the importance of such actions?
Of course, my child. It's heartening to see how your aunt's kind actions have left a positive mark on the lives of others. The Bhagavad Gita teaches us about the importance of virtuous deeds, and I can share a shloka that might resonate with you.
puṇya-karmaṇāṁ lokān uṣhitvā śhāśhvatīḥ samāḥ
Śhūrāḥ śhūra-taram eva bhavanti
|| 10 ||
One who at the time of death, with unmoving mind attained by the practice of Yog, fixes the prāṇ (life-airs) between the eyebrows, and steadily remembers the Divine Lord with great devotion, certainly attains Him.

The shloka teaches us that by performing meritorious actions, individuals can attain higher realms and lasting happiness. Just as your aunt's actions have brought comfort and joy to those she helped, virtuous deeds lead to both personal progress and the betterment of society.
So, by doing good deeds, we not only make others happy but also improve our own lives?

Absolutely. Acts of kindness, charity, and generosity create a positive ripple effect. They bring happiness to those who receive your help and also elevate your own spirit. Just like your aunt's actions have left a positive legacy, our virtuous deeds contribute to a better world and uplift our own consciousness.
That's amazing, Guruji. It inspires me to do good things for others too.

Guruji, do you think my aunt will be born again? Will she have to go through this cycle of life and death again?
Those are profound questions, my child. According to spiritual beliefs, the cycle of birth and rebirth, known as samsara, is a fundamental concept. Souls go through multiple births until they achieve liberation or moksha.
BHAGAVAD GITA
But Guruji, isn't it tiring to keep on going through this cycle? Will we have to do this in every birth?
Let me share a shloka from The Bhagavad Gita that might help you understand this better.
mām upetya punar janma duḥkhālayam aśāśvatam
nāpnuvanti mahātmānaḥ saṁsiddhiṁ paramāṁ gatāḥ
|| 15 ||
Having attained Me, the great souls are no more subject to rebirth in this world, which is transient and full of misery, because they have attained the highest perfection.

The Bhagavad Gita explains that those who attain the supreme realization, who achieve union with the divine, do not need to undergo rebirth in this temporary world of suffering. Such enlightened souls have reached the pinnacle of spiritual evolution.
That sounds amazing, Guruji. So, if we do enough good deeds and grow spiritually, we can also escape this cycle?

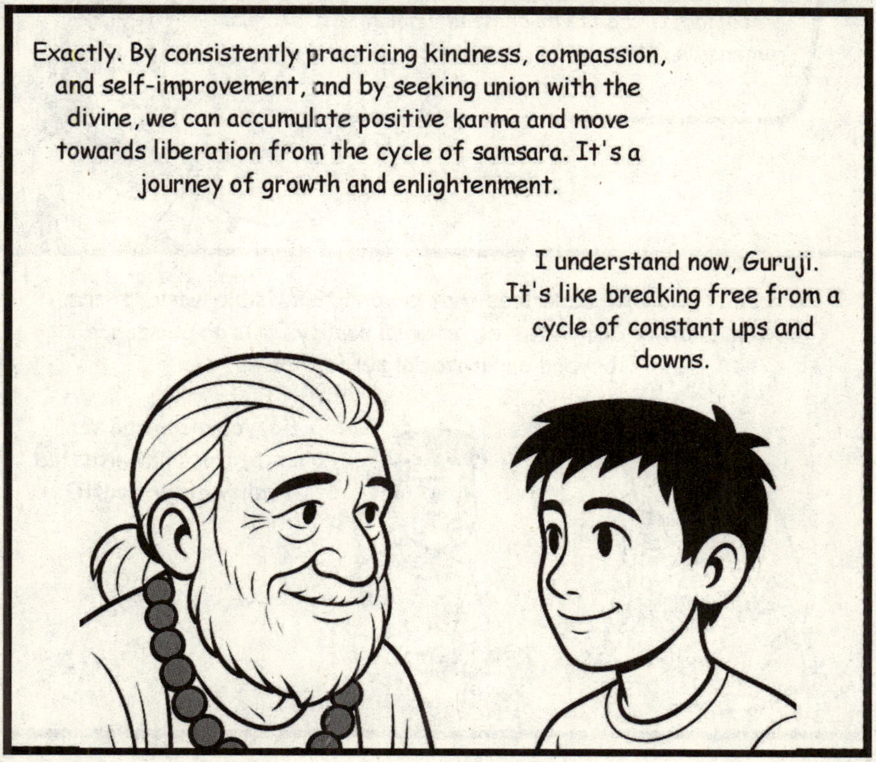
Exactly. By consistently practicing kindness, compassion, and self-improvement, and by seeking union with the divine, we can accumulate positive karma and move towards liberation from the cycle of samsara. It's a journey of growth and enlightenment.
I understand now, Guruji. It's like breaking free from a cycle of constant ups and downs.

Guruji, where does the soul of people go after they die?
Ah, that's a profound question, my young seeker. According to spiritual beliefs, the soul embarks on a journey after death. Here's a shloka from Bhagavad Gita that might help you understand the concept of rebirth.

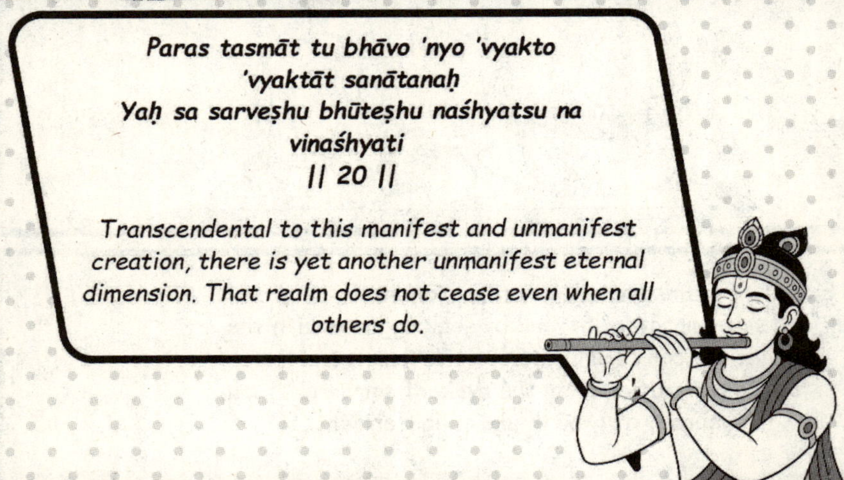
Paras tasmāt tu bhāvo 'nyo 'vyakto
'vyaktāt sanātanaḥ
Yaḥ sa sarveṣhu bhūteṣhu naśhyatsu na
vinaśhyati
|| 20 ||
Transcendental to this manifest and unmanifest creation, there is yet another unmanifest eternal dimension. That realm does not cease even when all others do.

The Bhagavad Gita describes that beyond this visible world, there exists another unmanifested, eternal reality. It is an existence beyond our material perception.
So, you mean the soul goes to this unmanifested reality after death?

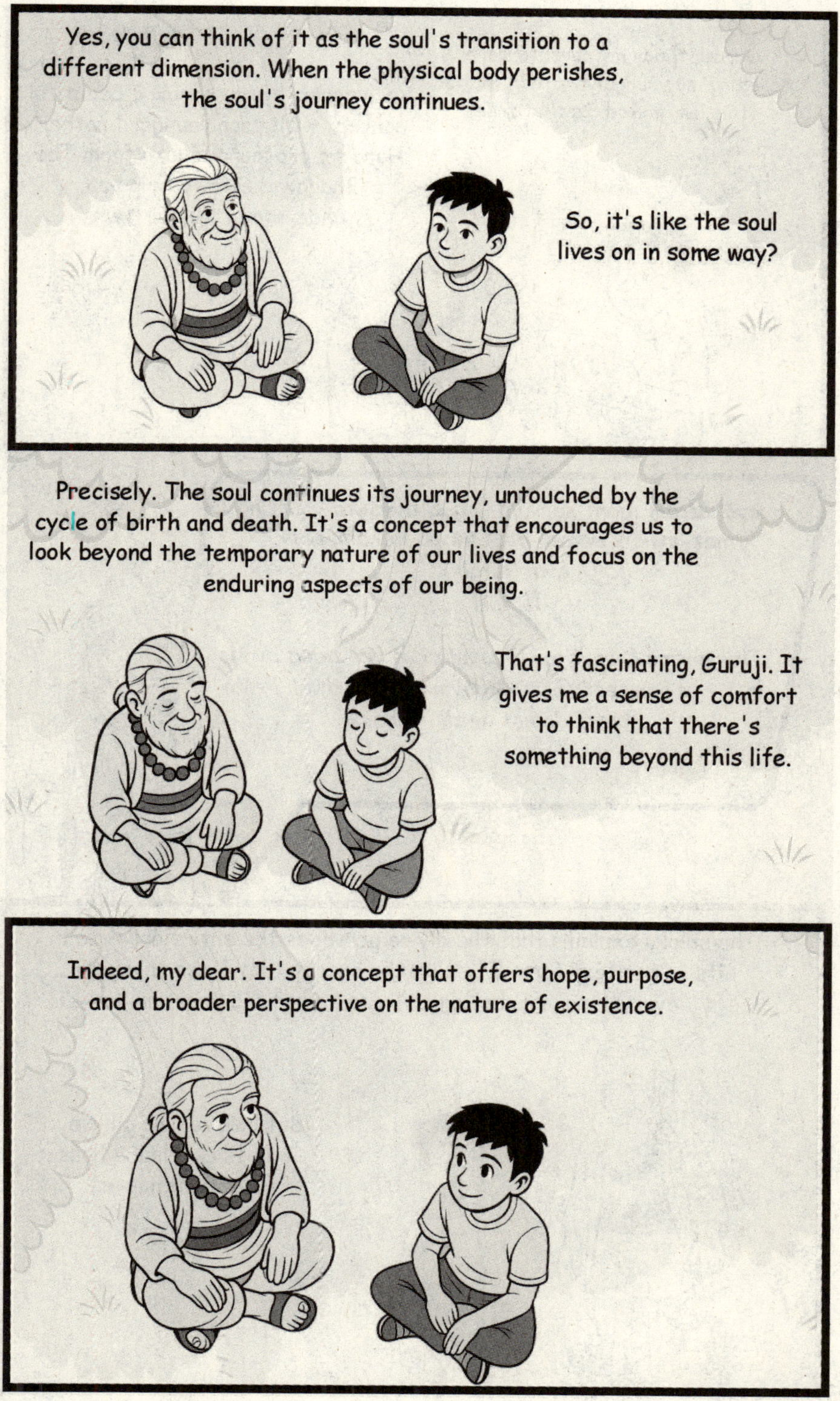
Yes, you can think of it as the soul's transition to a different dimension. When the physical body perishes, the soul's journey continues.
So, it's like the soul lives on in some way?
Precisely. The soul continues its journey, untouched by the cycle of birth and death. It's a concept that encourages us to look beyond the temporary nature of our lives and focus on the enduring aspects of our being.
That's fascinating, Guruji. It gives me a sense of comfort to think that there's something beyond this life.
Indeed, my dear. It's a concept that offers hope, purpose, and a broader perspective on the nature of existence.

Adhyaya 9
Guruji, today my parents were teaching my younger brother that all of us live in God. Is that true?
Your parents are sharing a beautiful concept with your younger brother. Here's a profound shloka from The Bhagavad Gita to help you understand this better:
mayā tatam idaṁ sarvaṁ jagad avyakta-mūrtinā
mat-sthāni sarva-bhūtāni na cāhaṁ teṣv avasthitaḥ
|| 4 ||
This entire cosmic manifestation is pervaded by Me in My unmanifest form. All living beings dwell in Me, but I do not dwell in them.
The shloka explains that the divine pervades the entire universe in its unmanifest form. It's like the energy that flows through everything, connecting all living beings and creation.
But how can we all live in God? Is God like a house that contains us?

The shloka tells us that unintelligent people might think of the divine as having taken a human form. However, they don't fully understand the higher, eternal, and supreme nature of the divine.
So, does that mean god cannot take a human form?
It's not about what god can or cannot do, but rather about our understanding and perception. The divine is beyond human comprehension, and while some may believe in manifestations of the divine in human form, it's important to also explore the higher truths and eternal nature of the divine. Spirituality is a journey of seeking higher truths and connecting with the divine in ways that resonate with your heart and soul. Keep an open mind and explore the vastness of spirituality.
Thank you, Guruji. This helps me a lot.

Guruji, if we all live in God, how come some people hurt others, like thieves and cheaters?
That's a thought-provoking question, Boy. The Bhagavad Gita has a shloka just about this.
BHAGAVAD GITA
moghasa mogha-karmano mogha-jnana vicetasah
raksasim asurim caiva prakrtim mohinim sritah
|| 12 ||
Bewildered by the material energy, such persons embrace demoniac and atheistic views. In that deluded state, their hopes for welfare are in vain, their fruitive actions are wasted, and their culture of knowledge is baffled.
It talks about those who lack discrimination, whose actions are futile, and whose knowledge is shallow. They are drawn towards negative tendencies and behaviors.
So, some people might not realize the divine connection and make wrong choices?

Exactly. Lack of understanding, misguided intentions, or being clouded by negative influences can lead individuals to make harmful choices. The divine connection might be there, but it's the choices they make that determine their actions.
But wouldn't they feel bad hurting others if they knew we're all connected through the divine?
Ideally, yes. Recognizing the interconnectedness and the divine presence in all beings can cultivate empathy and compassion. However, people can sometimes become disconnected from their higher nature due to various reasons.
So, what can we do to help them see the connection and make better choices?
We can lead by example, boy. By living with compassion, understanding, and integrity, we can inspire others to recognize their own divine nature and choose actions that promote harmony and well-being.
That sounds great! I'll live a life full of compassion, understanding, and integrity so I would contribute to a more compassionate and harmonious world.

Guruji, you mentioned that some people are drawn to negative behaviors. But what makes them do so?
Ah, that's an insightful question, Boy. Often, it's our desires and attachments that influence our choices and actions.
Desires and attachments? How do they play a role in this?
This shloka explains it beautifully.
te tam bhuktva svarga-lokam visalam ksine
punye martya-lokam visanti
evam trayi-dharmam anuprapanna
gatagatam kama-kama labhante
|| 21 ||
When they have enjoyed the vast pleasures of heaven, the stock of their merits being exhausted, they return to the earthly plane. Thus, those who follow the Vedic rituals, desiring objects of enjoyment, repeatedly come and go in this world.

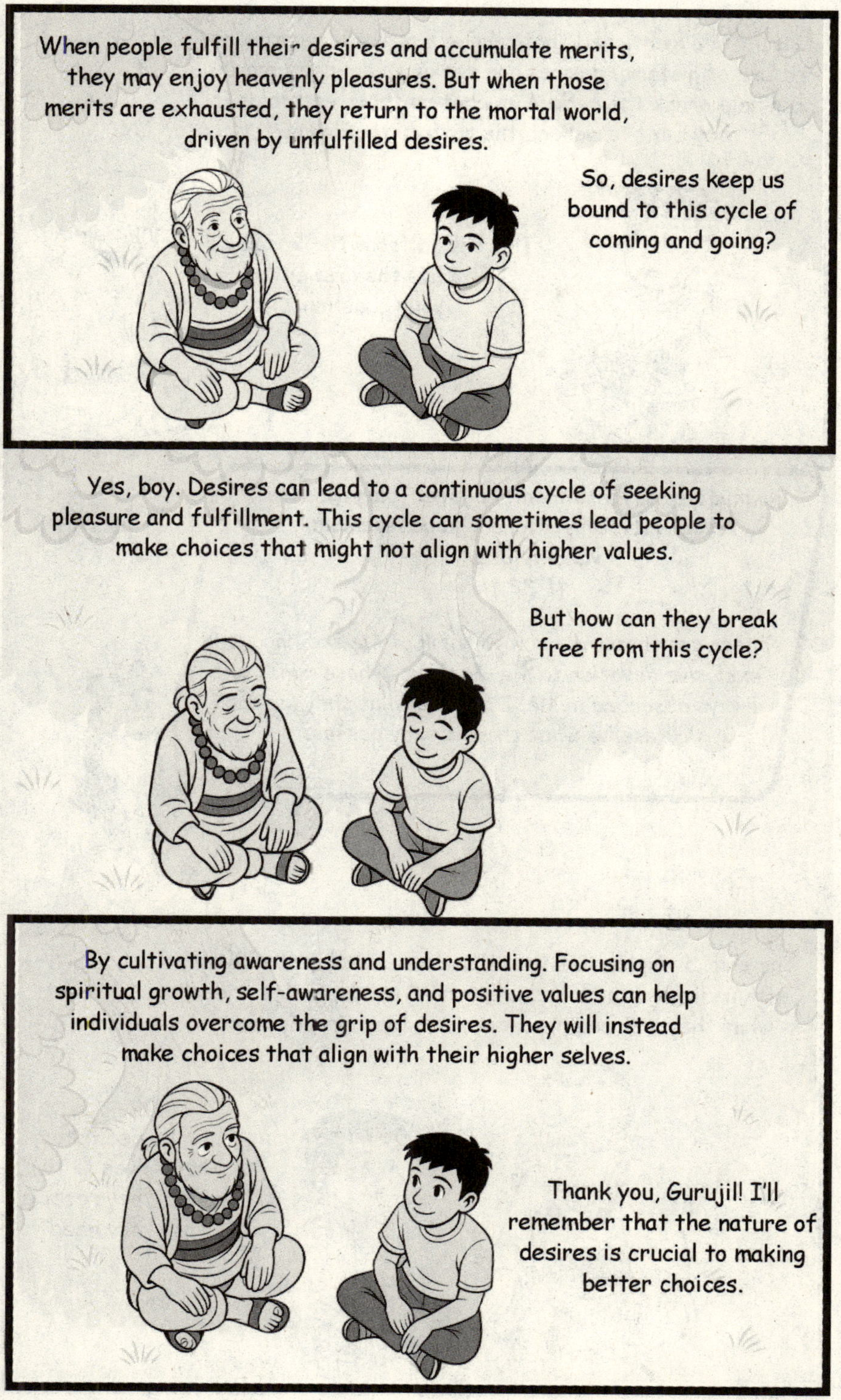
When people fulfill their desires and accumulate merits, they may enjoy heavenly pleasures. But when those merits are exhausted, they return to the mortal world, driven by unfulfilled desires.
So, desires keep us bound to this cycle of coming and going?
Yes, boy. Desires can lead to a continuous cycle of seeking pleasure and fulfillment. This cycle can sometimes lead people to make choices that might not align with higher values.
But how can they break free from this cycle?
By cultivating awareness and understanding. Focusing on spiritual growth, self-awareness, and positive values can help individuals overcome the grip of desires. They will instead make choices that align with their higher selves.
Thank you, Gurujil! I'll remember that the nature of desires is crucial to making better choices.

Guruji, you mentioned that recognizing the impermanent nature of material desires and seeking a deeper purpose can help break the cycle. But what do they need to do if they want to walk on the path of the divine?
This shloka from The Bhagavad Gita has the answer to your question.
ananyāś cintayanto māṁ ye janāḥ paryupāsate
teṣāṁ nityābhiyuktānāṁ yoga-kṣemaṁ vahāmy aham
|| 22 ||
There are those who always think of Me and engage in exclusive devotion to Me. To them, whose minds are always absorbed in Me, I provide what they lack and preserve what they already possess.
The shloka emphasizes that those who worship the divine with undivided focus and unwavering minds, God provide what they lack and preserve what they already have.
So, by dedicating themselves to the divine, they receive what they need?

Yes, Boy. When one's heart and mind are completely dedicated to the divine, they find that their material needs are taken care of. The divine understands their true desires and guides them on their journey.
How can someone dedicate themselves like that?

By cultivating a deep sense of connection and love for the divine, Boy. Through regular practices like prayer, meditation, and acts of kindness, individuals can establish a strong bond with the divine.
When people walk the path of the divine, they receive the support and guidance they need to overcome challenges, find inner peace, and fulfill their true purpose.
It sounds like a beautiful journey of focusing on the divine and letting go of other distractions.

Guruji, when one prays to God, is there anything that God expects in return?
Your question reminds me of a beautiful shloka. It goes like this:
patram puspam phalam toyam yo me bhaktya prayacchati
tad aham bhakty-upahrtam asnami prayatatmanah
|| 26 ||
If one offers to Me with devotion a leaf, a flower, a fruit, or even water, I delightfully partake of that item offered with love by My devotee in pure consciousness.

It means that whatever is offered to God with devotion, God accepts it with a heart full of devotion. So, it's not about material things. God values the love, sincerity, and devotion with which we offer anything. It's about the intention behind the offering.
So, it's not about the value of the offering, but the love we put into it?

Exactly, Boy. God doesn't measure offerings by their material worth. What truly matters is the love and devotion that accompany the offering.
That's a wonderful way to think about it.

Guruji, when someone is devoted to God, what does God do for them?
I'll let this shloka from The Bhagavad Gita answer your curious question.
ksipram bhavati dharmatma sasvac-chantim nigacchati
kaunteya pratijanihi na me bhaktah pranasyati
|| 31 ||
Quickly they become virtuous, and attain lasting peace. O son of Kunti, declare it boldly that no devotee of Mine is ever lost.

When someone dedicates themselves to righteousness and devotion, they find inner transformation and lasting peace. It's a reminder that when we align ourselves with the divine, we receive support and guidance on our path.
That's comforting to know. So, God is there to guide and protect those who are devoted?

Absolutely, Boy. God's grace is always with those who strive for goodness and walk the path of devotion. It's a source of strength and assurance on our spiritual journey.

Guruji, what about those who are born in conditions they have no control over, like unfavorable circumstances or lowly positions in society? Does God treat them the same as every other devotee?
There's a shloka that talks exactly about this.

mam hi partha vyapasritya ye 'pi syuh papa-yonayah
striyo vaisyas tatha sudras te 'pi yanti param gatim
|| 32 ||
All those who take refuge in Me, whatever their birth, race, gender, or caste, even those whom society scorns, will attain the supreme destination.

Guruji, how would I know if I'm praying to God correctly?
A thoughtful question, my dear. Let me share with you a shloka from the Bhagavad Gita that might shed some light on this.
udarah sarva evaite jncni tv atmaiva me matam
asthitah sa hi yuktatma mam evanuttamam gatim
|| 18 ||
All those who are devoted to Me are indeed noble. But those in knowledge, who are of steadfast mind, whose intellect is merged in Me and who have made Me alone as their supreme goal, I consider as My very self.
The shloka tells us that all individuals who possess nobility, wisdom, and devotion are dear to the divine. But the one who is not only virtuous but also steadfastly united with the divine within themselves, that person is considered to have reached the ultimate destination.
So, it's not just about reciting prayers?

Adhyaya 10
Guruji, today we took my little brother to the temple for the first time. We told him that God lives there. Is it true?
It's a beautiful sentiment to think of temples as places where we connect with the divine, my young friend. Many people believe that God's presence can be felt strongly in places of worship. The idea of God's presence in temples is based on faith and devotion. People find solace, guidance, and a sense of connection to the divine by visiting temples.
So, you're saying God might not actually live in the temple?
The concept of the divine is much more intricate than we can fully comprehend. Just like the shloka from the Bhagavad Gita says;
na me viduḥ sura-gaṇāḥ prabhavaṁ na maharṣhayaḥ
aham ādir hi devānāṁ maharṣhīṇāṁ cha sarvaśhaḥ
|| 2 ||
Neither celestial gods nor the great sages know of My origin. I am the source from which the gods and great seers come.

The shloka suggests that even the greatest sages and celestial beings don't entirely know the origin of the divine. It's a mystery that goes beyond our human understanding.
So, we don't know if God lives in the temple or not?
What we do know is that temples hold significance as places of reverence and spiritual practice. They offer us an opportunity to connect with something beyond ourselves, to find peace, and to seek answers to life's questions.
That makes sense, Guruji. I guess it's more about what we feel when we're there.
Exactly. The temple becomes a space where we can cultivate devotion, introspection, and a sense of unity with the divine. It's about the experience and the connection, rather than just a physical location.
Thank you, Guruji. I feel like I understand better now.

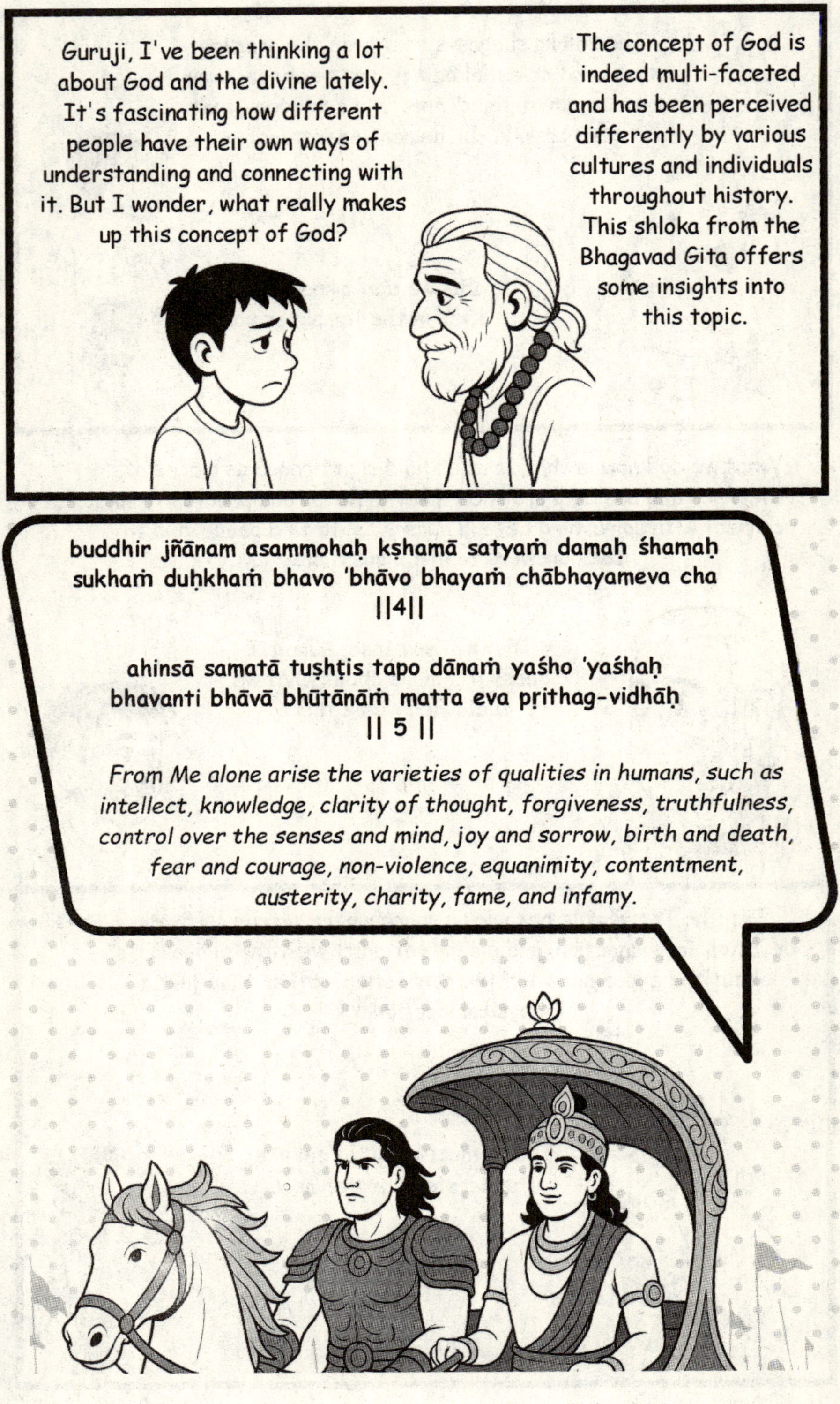
Guruji, I've been thinking a lot about God and the divine lately. It's fascinating how different people have their own ways of understanding and connecting with it. But I wonder, what really makes up this concept of God?
The concept of God is indeed multi-faceted and has been perceived differently by various cultures and individuals throughout history. This shloka from the Bhagavad Gita offers some insights into this topic.
buddhir jñānam asammohaḥ kṣhamā satyaṁ damaḥ śhamaḥ
sukhaṁ duḥkhaṁ bhavo 'bhāvo bhayaṁ chābhayameva cha
||4||
ahinsā samatā tuṣhṭis tapo dānaṁ yaśho 'yaśhaḥ
bhavanti bhāvā bhūtānāṁ matta eva pṛithag-vidhāḥ
|| 5 ||
From Me alone arise the varieties of qualities in humans, such as intellect, knowledge, clarity of thought, forgiveness, truthfulness, control over the senses and mind, joy and sorrow, birth and death, fear and courage, non-violence, equanimity, contentment, austerity, charity, fame, and infamy.

This shloka lists a wide range of qualities and experiences, all of which are said to be created by the divine.
So, these qualities are like pieces of a puzzle that form the bigger picture of God?

You could say that, indeed. The divine is often described as the source of virtues like forgiveness, self-control, and truthfulness. Equally, the experiences of pleasure and pain, birth and death, fear and fearlessness—all these are part of the broader spectrum of life that we associate with the divine's creation.
Thank you, Guruji. This shloka has given me a new perspective on how the divine is present in every aspect of our lives.

Guruji, I've been pondering over something. You mentioned that all these qualities and experiences are created by God. Does that mean that God is only concerned with what happens on Earth?
Ah, an insightful question, my young friend. The Bhagavad Gita has a shloka about this that actually presents a broader perspective about this.
sargāṇām ādir antaśh cha madhyaṁ chaivāham arjuna
adhyātma-vidyā vidyānāṁ vādaḥ pravadatām aham
|| 32 ||
O Arjun, know Me to be the beginning, middle, and end of all creation. Amongst sciences I am the science of spirituality, and in debates I am the logical conclusion.
Let me explain. The shloka states that God is the beginning, the end, and the middle of all creations. This doesn't just refer to Earth—it encompasses the entire universe and beyond. Just as life has a beginning, middle, and end, the divine essence is present throughout the entire cosmic journey. From the tiniest particle to the vast expanse of galaxies, the divine is the underlying force that sustains it all.
It's like the divine is the thread that connects everything in the universe.

You've captured it beautifully, my dear. Additionally, the shloka mentions that among all sciences, the spiritual science of the Self is the most profound. This signifies that the divine is not only concerned with the physical world but also guides us in understanding the essence of our own being.
And what about the conclusive truth among logicians?
In the realm of knowledge and understanding, the divine represents the ultimate truth. Just as a logical argument reaches a conclusive point, the divine essence represents the ultimate reality and wisdom that underlies all things.
Thank you, Guruji. Your explanation helps me see that the divine is not limited by time, space, or even Earth. It's a part of everything in the universe.

Adhyaya 11
Guruji, you mentioned that God is the beginning, middle, and end of everything. Then why do my parents go to the temple every day to pray? Can't they simply pray at home since God is everywhere?
BHAGAVAD GITA
Yes, God's presence is indeed everywhere, just as you've understood. But going to a temple or a place of worship holds a deeper significance.
bhaktyā tv ananyayā śhakya aham evaṁ-vidho 'rjuna
jñātuṁ draṣhṭuṁ cha tattvena praveṣhṭuṁ cha parantapa
|| 54 ||
O Arjun, by unalloyed devotion alone can I be known as I am, standing before you. Thereby, on receiving My divine vision, O scorcher of foes, one can enter into union with Me.
The shloka teaches us that the divine can be understood only by undivided devotional service. Only in this way can one enter into the mysteries of the divine's understanding.
Temples are spaces where people come together to focus their thoughts, prayers, and devotion. It's not just about asking for things, but also about connecting with the divine in a concentrated and meaningful way.
But can't they do that at home too?

Of course, my dear. The divine can be reached from anywhere, and heartfelt prayers are always heard. However, visiting a temple offers a chance to step away from the hustle and bustle of daily life.
So, it's like making a conscious effort to strengthen that connection?
Exactly. Just as the shloka I mentioned earlier says, by undivided devotional service, we can truly understand and experience the divine. Visiting a temple is a form of undivided devotion, a way to strengthen the bond with the divine.

Guruji, I've come to understand the importance of going to the temple and connecting with the divine. I want to help my younger brother understand this too. Can you guide me on how to teach him about the significance of devotional services?
Of course, my dear. Teaching your younger brother about the importance of devotional services is a wonderful endeavor. Remember, teaching by example is often the most effective way.
मत्कर्मकृन्मत्परमो मद्भक्तः सङ्गवर्जितः |
निर्वैरः सर्वभूतेषु यः स मामेति पाण्डव
|| 55 ||
Those who perform all their duties for My sake, who depend upon Me and are devoted to Me, who are free from attachment, and are without malice toward all beings, such devotees certainly come to Me.
You can start by encouraging him to cultivate a positive and compassionate attitude towards all living beings. Just as the shloka mentions being friendly to every living entity, teach him to be kind and considerate to animals, plants, and people alike.
That's a great idea, Guruji. What about going to the temple?

You can take him to the temple occasionally and explain to him that it's a place where people come to offer their prayers and gratitude to the divine. Tell him stories from scriptures that emphasize the values of love, compassion, and devotion.
And what about rituals and practices?

Introduce simple rituals like lighting a lamp or offering a flower to the divine. Explain to him that these rituals are ways of expressing our love and respect for the divine presence. However, also help him understand that the true essence lies in the sincerity of the heart.
Thank you, Guruji. I will do my best to guide him with these teachings.

Adhyaya 12
Guruji, when we go to the temple, what should we keep in mind during worship, and who should we worship?
Let me share a shloka that will guide you on this journey of devotion.
mayy āveśhya mano ye māṁ nitya-yuktā upāsate
śhraddhayā parayopetās te me yuktatamā matāḥ
|| 2 ||
The Lord said: Those who fix their minds on Me and always engage in My devotion with steadfast faith, I consider them to be the best yogis
This shloka from the Bhagavad Gita tells us that those who worship the unmanifested, the divine presence that lies beyond the perception of our senses, achieve the highest level of devotion. They cultivate unwavering faith, meditating on the all-pervading, inconceivable, and unchanging nature of the Absolute Truth.
So, we should focus on something greater than what we can see or touch?

Exactly. When you worship with a mind that is focused on the divine, you're connecting with a higher reality that goes beyond the physical world. It's a way to seek something profound and eternal.
But how should we treat others while we're on this path?

The shloka also teaches us about treating everyone with equality and kindness. When you're able to see the divine presence in every being, your heart becomes a wellspring of compassion and love. Treating others with respect and kindness is an essential part of worship.
Thank you, Guruji. I'll keep this in mind the next time I visit the temple.

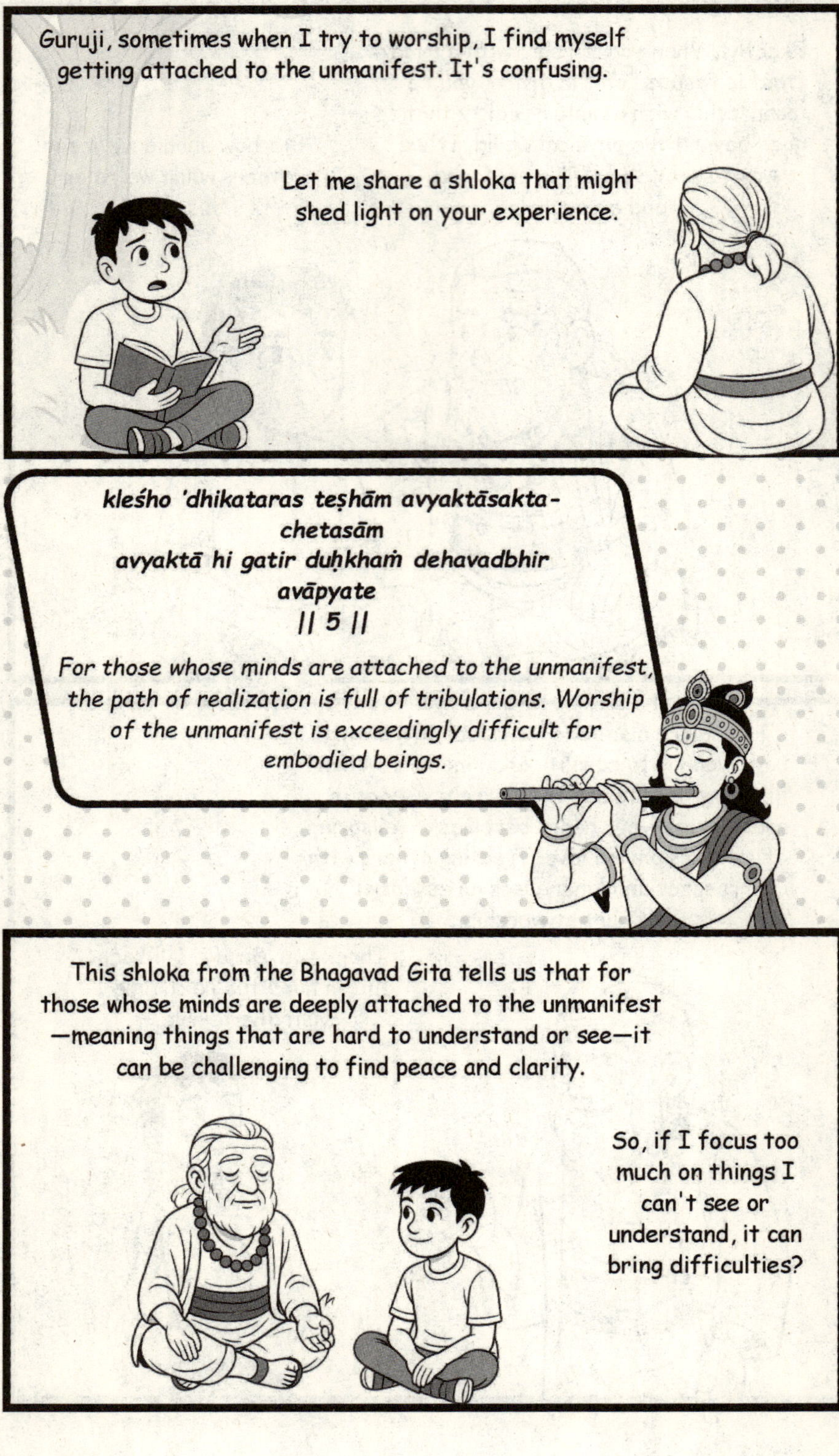

Guruji, sometimes when I try to worship, I find myself getting attached to the unmanifest. It's confusing.
Let me share a shloka that might shed light on your experience.
kleśho 'dhikataras teṣhām avyaktāsakta-chetasām
avyaktā hi gatir duḥkhaṁ dehavadbhir avāpyate
|| 5 ||
For those whose minds are attached to the unmanifest, the path of realization is full of tribulations. Worship of the unmanifest is exceedingly difficult for embodied beings.
This shloka from the Bhagavad Gita tells us that for those whose minds are deeply attached to the unmanifest—meaning things that are hard to understand or see—it can be challenging to find peace and clarity.
So, if I focus too much on things I can't see or understand, it can bring difficulties?

Exactly. Sometimes, when we spend too much time thinking about things that are beyond our grasp, it can lead to confusion and even sadness. So, focus on the things that are more tangible and understandable. Enjoy the beauty of nature, cherish the love of your family, and delight in learning new things.
So, instead of getting lost in things I don't fully understand, I should appreciate the simpler things around me?

Precisely. When you shift your focus to the things you can experience and appreciate, your journey becomes smoother and more joyful.
Thank you, Guruji. I'll remember this the next time I feel tangled in confusing thoughts.

Guruji, What do you think God values in His favorite children?
There's a shloka from the Bhagavad Gita that speaks directly to your question.
yasmān nodvijate loko lokān nodvijate cha yaḥ
harṣhāmarṣha-bhayodvegair mukto yaḥ sa cha
me priyaḥ
|| 15 ||
Those who are not a source of annoyance to anyone and who in turn are not agitated by anyone, who are equal in pleasure and pain, and free from fear and anxiety, such devotees of Mine are very dear to Me.
It says, "One who is not perturbed by the world and is not perturbing the world, and who remains unaffected by joy, anger, fear, and anxiety - such a person is dear to Me."
So, to be God's favorite, I should stay calm in all situations and not let emotions like joy, anger, fear, and anxiety affect me?

Exactly. When you're able to maintain inner peace and emotional balance, you create a positive and harmonious atmosphere around you. Just as you said, not causing trouble for others is also important. Treat everyone with kindness and respect, and your actions will reflect the qualities that God cherishes.
But how can I achieve that? Sometimes it's hard not to get upset.

It's natural to feel emotions, my child. The key is to observe them without being controlled by them. When joy, anger, fear, or anxiety arise, acknowledge them, but don't let them dictate your actions. With practice, you'll find it easier to maintain a calm and ba anced state of mind.
Thank you, Guruji. I'll do my best to stay calm and treat everyone kindly.

Adhyaya 13
Guruji, I've heard so many people say that God is present everywhere. Is that true?
Imagine, my dear, that the world around us is like a vast field where different elements and forces are at play. Just like a field where various plants grow, our world is composed of different components that interact with each other.
So, you mean everything in the world is connected somehow?
Absolutely. Just as a field has soil, water, air, and sunlight that help plants grow, our world consists of five great elements - earth, water, fire, air, and ether - that interact to create everything around us.
But what about God? Is God a part of this field too?
In a way, yes. God's presence can be found in the very essence of creation. The shloka from the Bhagavad Gita tells us that everything is interconnected and influenced by divine energy.

mahā-bhūtāny ahankāro buddhir avyaktam eva cha
indriyāṇi daśhaikaṁ cha pañcha chendriya-gocharāḥ
|| 6 ||
The field of activities is composed of the five great elements, the ego, the intellect, the unmanifest primordial matter, the eleven senses (five knowledge senses, five working senses, and mind), and the five objects of the senses.
So, God is present in everything, like the soil, water, air, and sunlight in a field?
Exactly. God's presence is like the invisible thread that weaves through the fabric of creation. Just as the sun's rays touch every corner of the field, God's energy is present in every aspect of our world, guiding and nurturing it.
That's amazing! So, when I see the world around me, I can remember that God's presence is there too.

Guruji, if God is present everywhere, does it mean that He sees everything that happens anywhere?
Imagine, my dear, that God's presence is like the light of the sun that shines upon every corner of the world. Just as the sun's rays touch every object, God's awareness is present in all places.

So, God sees everything that happens?
Yes, in a sense. There is a shloka from The Bhagavad Gita that says "Everywhere are His hands and feet, eyes, heads, and faces. His ears too are in all places, for He pervades everything in the universe."

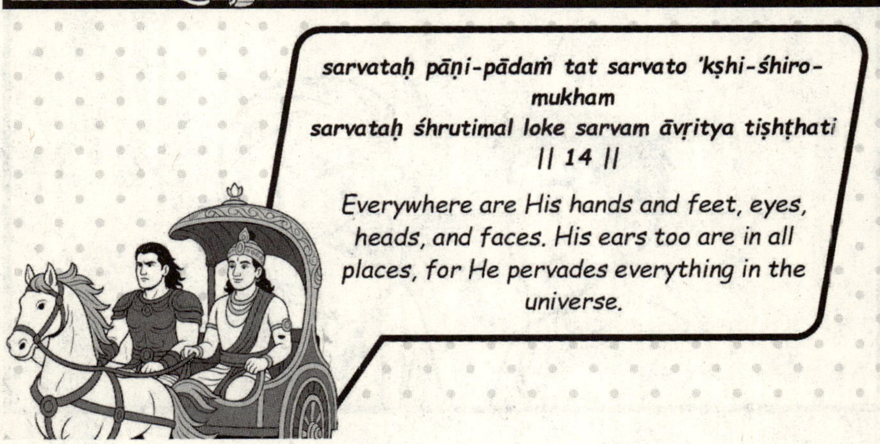
sarvataḥ pāṇi-pādaṁ tat sarvato 'kṣhi-śhiro-mukham
sarvataḥ śhrutimal loke sarvam āvṛitya tiṣhṭhati || 14 ||
Everywhere are His hands and feet, eyes, heads, and faces. His ears too are in all places, for He pervades everything in the universe.

That's amazing! So, God is aware of all the good and bad things that happen?
God's awareness is like a vast and boundless ocean. But remember, my dear, that God's awareness is not limited by human concepts of good or bad. It's a presence that encourages us to live with integrity and compassion.
So, when I do something, God's presence is there too?
Absolutely. God's presence is within you and around you, guiding you toward goodness. Just as you feel the warmth of the sun's rays, you can sense God's guidance in your heart and conscience.
That's comforting. It means that I'm never alone, and I should always strive to do what's right. Thank you for explaining it to me!

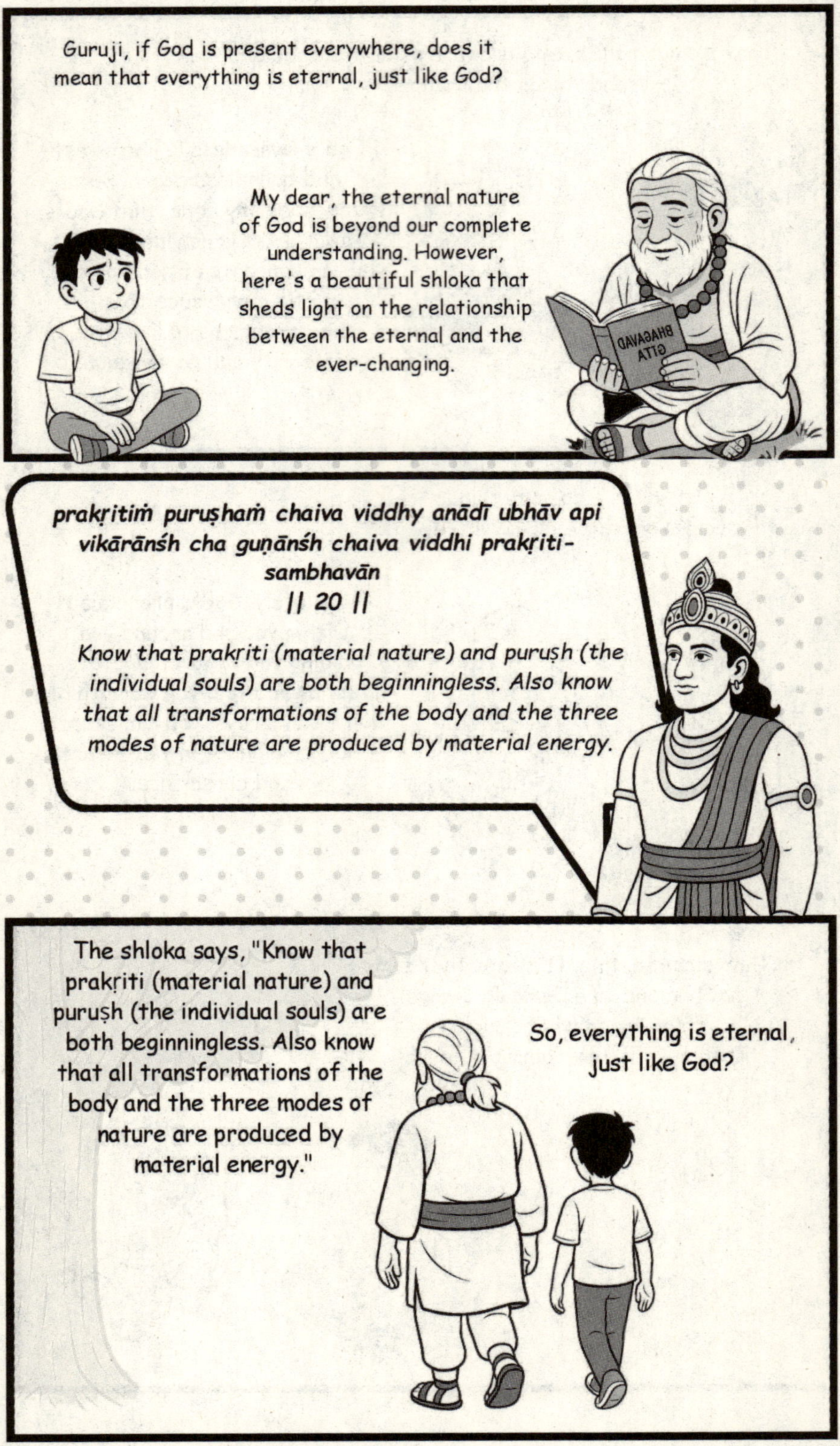

Guruji, if God is present everywhere, does it mean that everything is eternal, just like God?
My dear, the eternal nature of God is beyond our complete understanding. However, here's a beautiful shloka that sheds light on the relationship between the eternal and the ever-changing.
prakṛitiṁ puruṣhaṁ chaiva viddhy anādī ubhāv api
vikārānśh cha guṇānśh chaiva viddhi prakṛiti-sambhavān
|| 20 ||
Know that prakṛiti (material nature) and puruṣh (the individual souls) are both beginningless. Also know that all transformations of the body and the three modes of nature are produced by material energy.
The shloka says, "Know that prakṛiti (material nature) and puruṣh (the individual souls) are both beginningless. Also know that all transformations of the body and the three modes of nature are produced by material energy."
So, everything is eternal, just like God?

Everything in this world, my dear, is a part of the eternal cycle of creation, preservation, and transformation. Just as a tree grows, bears fruit, and eventually returns to the earth, everything in nature undergoes change. But at the same time, the essence, the energy that sustains everything, remains eternal.
So, the changing forms are like waves in the eternal ocean?

Exactly! Just as waves rise and fall in the ocean, the forms in the world come and go. Yet, the ocean remains unchanged beneath it all. Similarly, God's eternal presence is like the unchanging ocean, while the world and its forms are like the waves of creation and transformation.
That's amazing, Guruji! It means that everything is connected to God's eternal energy.

Guruji, today I was telling Raghav about how God is present everywhere and in everything, but he didn't know about it. Is it okay for someone to not know these things already?
My dear, it's important to remember that everyone's spiritual journey is unique. Some people may not have encountered certain teachings or concepts yet, and that's perfectly okay. There is a shloka in The Bhagavad Gita about this.
anye tv evam ajānantaḥ śhrutvānyebhya upāsate
te 'pi chātitaranty eva mṛityuṁ śhruti-parāyaṇāḥ
|| 26 ||
There are still others who are unaware of these spiritual paths, but they hear from others and begin worshipping the Supreme Lord. By such devotion to hearing from saints, they too can gradually cross over the ocean of birth and death.
The shloka says: 'There are still others who are unaware of these spiritual paths, but they hear from others and begin worshipping the Supreme Lord. By such devotion to hearing from saints, they too can gradually cross over the ocean of birth and death.'
So, even if someone doesn't know, they can still learn and connect?

Absolutely. Just as a seed grows into a tree with the right nurturing, spiritual knowledge can also blossom when shared with an open heart. The joy lies in sharing what you've learned and in encouraging others to explore their own spiritual understanding.
Thank you, Guruji. I understand now that everyone's journey is different.

You're very wise, my dear. Remember, every step you take on your journey is valuable, and every opportunity to share your wisdom can make a positive impact on others.

Adhyaya 14
Guruji, I was playing Table Tennis with Raghav. The match got so intense that I completely forgot about my tuition classes.
Ah, let me share what The Bhagavad Gita has to say about this.

tamas tv ajnana-jam viddhi mohanam sarva-dehinam
pramadalasya-nidrabhis tan nibadhnati bharata
|| 8 ||
O Arjun, tamo guṇa, which is born of ignorance, is the cause of illusion for the embodied souls. It deludes all living beings through negligence, laziness, and sleep.

Guruji, I've been struggling lately. I love playing table tennis and studying, but it's getting hard to balance the two.
The challenge of finding balance between our passions is a common one. The Bhagavad Gita offers guidance on this very topic.
rajo ragatmakam viddhi trsna-sanga-samudbhavam
tan nibadhnati kaunteya karma-sangena dehinam
|| 7 ||
O Arjun, rajo guṇa is of the nature of passion. It arises from worldly desires and affections, and binds the soul through attachment to fruitive actions.
This shloka tells us about the mode of passion, rajas, which arises from attachment and leads to desire. It binds the soul through attachment to actions.
So, my passion for table tennis and studies, is that rajas?

Indeed. Passion is a driving force, but when it transforms into attachment and insatiable desires, it can create imbalance. If we let our passions dictate our actions without mindfulness, it can lead to conflicts.
So, I need to be mindful of my intentions and desires?

Exactly! Balance comes when you're mindful of your passions, nurturing them with dedication, yet maintaining detachment. This way, you'll enjoy both pursuits without losing your inner peace.
Thank you, Guruji. I'll remember this advice.

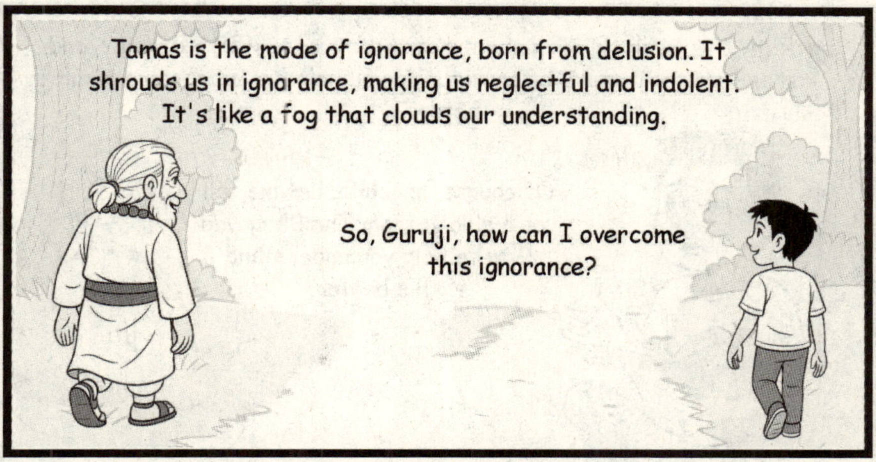

Remember, like a beam of sunlight clears away the fog, knowledge dispels ignorance. Just as you focus on the ball during a table tennis match, focus on your studies with the same dedication.

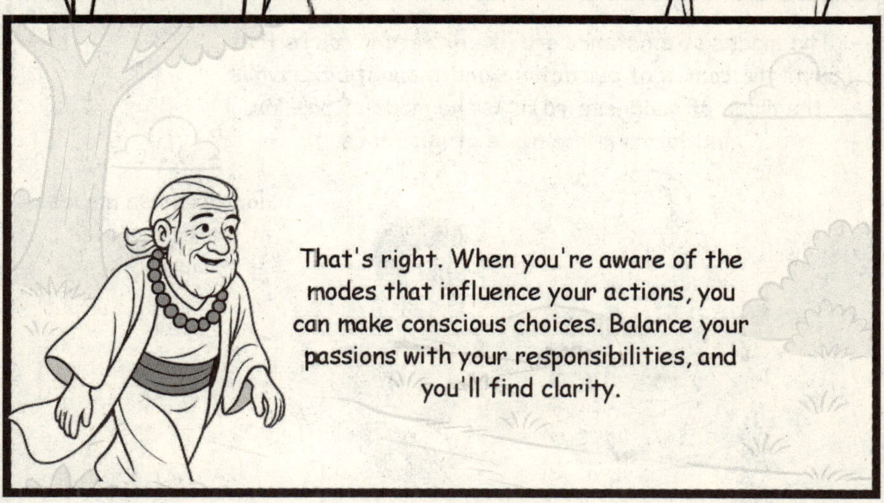

Guruji, I've been thinking about the three modes - sattva, rajas, and tamas - that you spoke of earlier. Can you help me understand them better?
Of course, my child. Let me tell you a shloka from The Bhagavad Gita to help you understand this better.

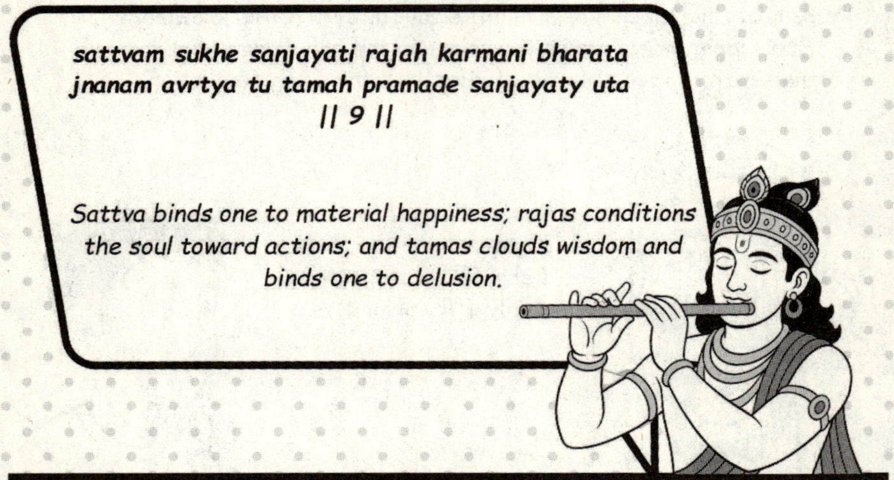
sattvam sukhe sanjayati rajah karmani bharata
jnanam avrtya tu tamah pramade sanjayaty uta
|| 9 ||
Sattva binds one to material happiness; rajas conditions the soul toward actions; and tamas clouds wisdom and binds one to delusion.

The modes of existence are like different colors that paint the canvas of our actions and thoughts. Sattva is the mode of goodness, rajas is the mode of passion, and tamas is the mode of ignorance.
How do these modes influence our lives, Guruji?

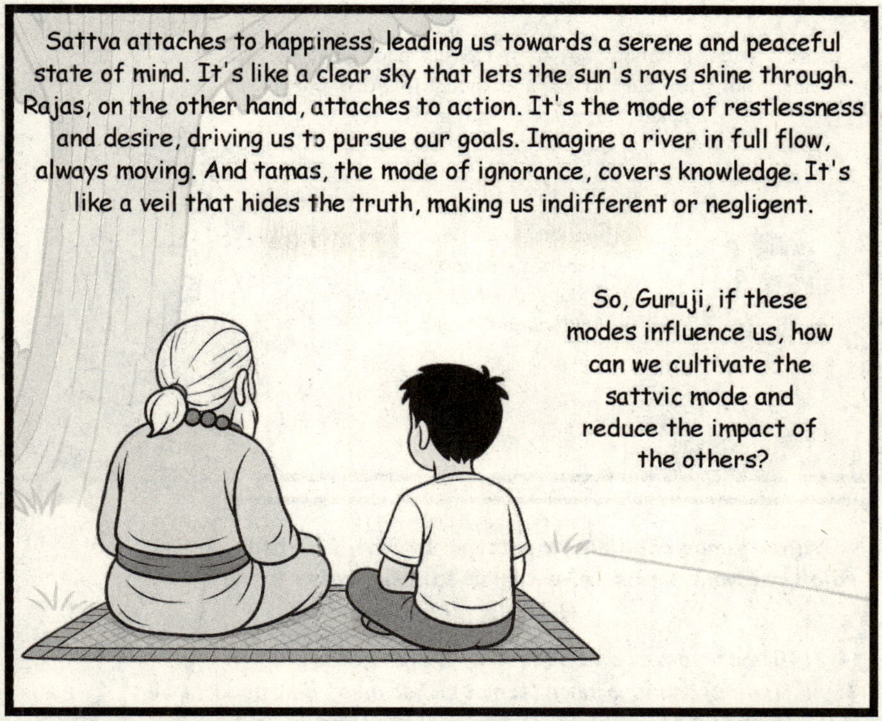
Sattva attaches to happiness, leading us towards a serene and peaceful state of mind. It's like a clear sky that lets the sun's rays shine through. Rajas, on the other hand, attaches to action. It's the mode of restlessness and desire, driving us to pursue our goals. Imagine a river in full flow, always moving. And tamas, the mode of ignorance, covers knowledge. It's like a veil that hides the truth, making us indifferent or negligent.
So, Guruji, if these modes influence us, how can we cultivate the sattvic mode and reduce the impact of the others?

Awareness, my child. Understanding the modes helps you recognize their influence. When you're mindful of your thoughts and actions, you can consciously choose the sattvic path. Engaging in selfless deeds, seeking knowledge, and practicing meditation can elevate your consciousness towards the mode of goodness.
Thank you, Guruji. Your guidance helps me see the colors of life more clearly now.

Guruji, you mentioned that sattva, rajas, and tamas are like colors that paint our actions and thoughts. But I'm curious, how do these modes actually arise?
Excellent question, my dear. Here's a shloka from The Bhagavad Gita to help you understand this better.
BHAGAVAD GITA
rajas tamas cabhibhuya sattvam bhavati bharata
rajah sattvam tamas caiva tamah sattvam rajas tatha
|| 10 ||
Sometimes goodness (sattva) prevails over passion (rajas) and ignorance (tamas), O scion of Bharat. Sometimes passion (rajas) dominates goodness (sattva) and ignorance (tamas), and at other times ignorance (tamas) overcomes goodness (sattva) and passion (rajas).
The modes are like currents in the ocean of existence. Let me explain. Imagine you're standing near a serene lake. The water is clear, and the surroundings are calm. This tranquility represents the mode of sattva.
I see. So, sattva arises when everything is peaceful and balanced?

Yes, exactly. Now, imagine a gust of wind rippling the lake's surface. The once-calm water now has waves and movement. This turbulence symbolizes the mode of rajas.
So, rajas arises when there's activity and restlessness?
Precisely. Now, think of a cloudy day when the sky is gray, and the world seems gloomy. This darkness represents the mode of tamas.
I think I'm starting to understand. But how do they interact and change?
You see, these modes are interconnected. Sattva arises by transcending rajas and tamas. When you overcome restlessness and ignorance, you find a state of peace and clarity. When you conquer rajas, both sattva and tamas emerge. By taming your excessive desires and actions, you can experience both clarity and stability. Similarly, by overcoming tamas, both sattva and rajas arise. Breaking free from ignorance and laziness leads to a balanced blend of activity and clarity.
Thank you, Guruji. Understanding this helps me see how they influence our choices and actions.

Guruji, you taught me about the three modes of material nature - sattva, rajas, and tamas. But what happens when someone rises above these modes?
Let me tell you what Krishna told Arjuna during The Mahabharata.
gunan etan atitya trin dehi deha-samudbhavan
janma-mrtyu-jara-duhkhair vimukto 'mrtam asnute
|| 20 ||
By transcending the three modes of material nature associated with the body, one becomes free from birth, death, old age, and misery, and attains immortality.
The shloka explains that when one transcends the influence of these modes, they attain a state of higher awareness and consciousness. It's like stepping into a realm beyond ordinary perceptions.
What does that lead to, Guruji?

By transcending these modes, the embodied soul becomes free from the cycle of birth, death, old age, and the pains that come with them. It's as if they've untangled themselves from the limitations of the material world.
So, they achieve immortality?

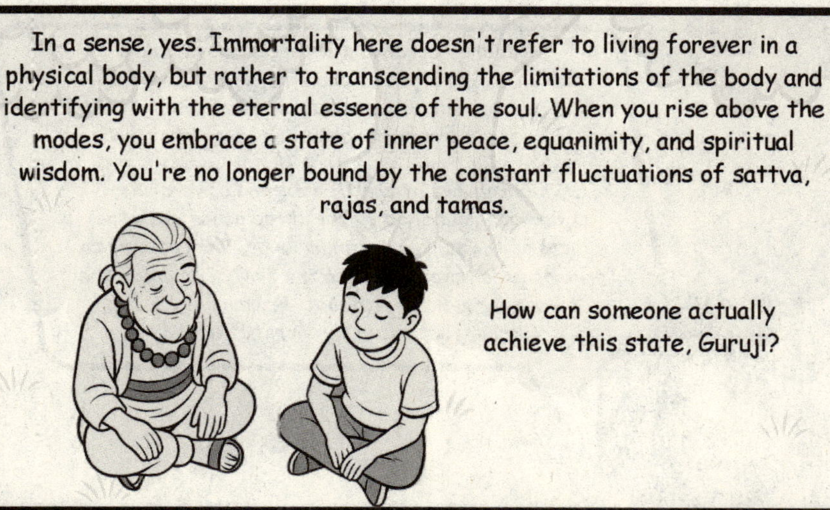
In a sense, yes. Immortality here doesn't refer to living forever in a physical body, but rather to transcending the limitations of the body and identifying with the eternal essence of the soul. When you rise above the modes, you embrace a state of inner peace, equanimity, and spiritual wisdom. You're no longer bound by the constant fluctuations of sattva, rajas, and tamas.
How can someone actually achieve this state, Guruji?

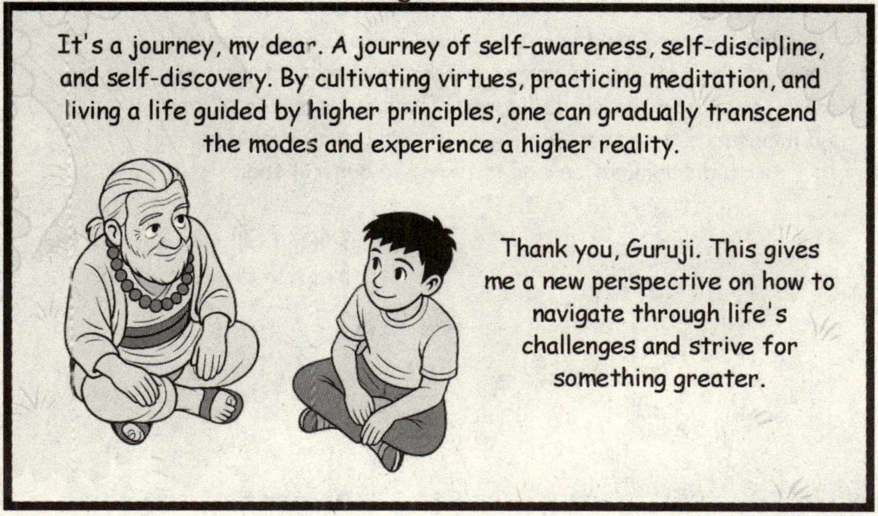
It's a journey, my dear. A journey of self-awareness, self-discipline, and self-discovery. By cultivating virtues, practicing meditation, and living a life guided by higher principles, one can gradually transcend the modes and experience a higher reality.
Thank you, Guruji. This gives me a new perspective on how to navigate through life's challenges and strive for something greater.

Adhyaya 15
Guruji, today I found it really difficult to focus in class. My mind kept wandering away from the lesson. I don't understand why.
You're not alone in this struggle. It happens to the best of us. Let me share a shloka with you that might shed some light on this.
adhas cordhvam prasrtas tasya sakha
guna-pravrddha visaya-pravalah
adhas ca mulany anusantatani
karmanubandhini manusya-loke
|| 2 ||
The branches of the tree extend upward and downward, nourished by the three guṇas, with the objects of the senses as tender buds. The roots of the tree hang downward, causing the flow of karma in the human form. Below, its roots branch out causing (karmic) actions in the world of humans.
Just as a strong wind can carry away a boat on water, even one of the roaming senses on which the mind focuses can carry away a person's intelligence. The senses are so strong and impetuous that they can forcibly carry away even a person with discrimination who is trying to control them.
So our mind will flow away in the direction of distraction?

Precisely. Your mind is like a boat, and the senses are like the wind. They can carry your thoughts away if you're not careful. It's normal to get distracted, but the key is to bring your focus back gently.
What can I do when I find myself getting distracted?
Whenever you notice your mind wandering, take a deep breath, acknowledge the distraction without judgment, and gently guide your thoughts back to the present moment. Over time, this practice will help you regain control over your focus.
Thank you for teaching this, Guruji. I'll definitely try it the next time I get distracted!

Guruji, I've been trying what you taught me about focusing my mind, and it's been really helping me in class. But I want to know, what else can I do to become wise?
Becoming wise is a journey that involves nurturing your inner qualities. There's a shloka from the Bhagavad Gita that guides us towards the qualities that lead to wisdom.
nirmana-moha jita-sanga-dosa adhyatma-nitya vinivrtta-kamah
dvandvair vimuktah sukha-duhkha-samjnair gacchanty amudhah padam avyayam tat
|| 5 ||
Those who are free from vanity and delusion, who have overcome the evil of attachment, who dwell constantly on the self and on God, who are free from the desire to enjoy the senses, and are beyond the dualities of pleasure and pain, such liberated personalities attain My eternal Abode.
It talks about being free from pride and delusion, being victorious over the evil of attachment, and being liberated from dualities such as pleasure and pain. Such people who are unattached to external things are considered wise and are able to reach their goal.
But Guruji, it's hard to control desires. They keep coming up.

It's natural to have desires, dear. The key is to have control over them, rather than letting them control you. When desires arise, observe them without acting on them immediately. Over time, you'll find that their hold weakens.
Lastly, being liberated from dualities like pleasure and pain means not letting your happiness depend on external circumstances. This inner stability helps you navigate through life's ups and downs with equanimity.
So, these qualities will make me wise?
Absolutely. Cultivating these qualities will not only make you wise but also bring a sense of peace and fulfillment. It's a journey, and every step you take towards these qualities will bring you closer to that imperishable goal of true wisdom.

Guruji, today some kids were making fun of the underprivileged kid. I went up to them and told them it's wrong. They ended up apologizing to the kid. Did I do the right thing?
You did something very commendable, Boy. Standing up against injustice and helping someone who's being treated unfairly is always the right thing to do.
But they were just having fun, and I felt like they didn't realize the impact of their words.
There's a shloka in The Bhagavad Gita that many people only perceive things on a surface level, without understanding the deeper aspects of a situation. It's like they have a materialistic vision that doesn't go beyond appearances.
utkramantam sthitam vapi bhunjanam va gunanvitam
vimudha nanupasyanti pasyanti jnana-caksusah
|| 10 ||
The ignorant do not perceive the soul as it resides in the body, and as it enjoys sense objects; nor do they perceive it when it departs. But those who possess the eyes of knowledge can behold it.

So, I guess I did the right thing by speaking up for the underprivileged kid.
Absolutely. Your action came from a place of empathy and understanding. You used the eye of knowledge, as mentioned in the shloka, to see beyond the surface and recognize the importance of treating others with kindness and respect.
Fairness and kindness are core values, Boy. And remember, your actions have the power to create positive ripples in the world. By standing up for what's right, you're not only helping the underprivileged kid but also inspiring others to do the same.
I just thought it was the fair thing to do.

Guruji, today I had lunch with the underprivileged kid at school. It felt really good to spend time with him because he was very calm. Can you tell me more about the importance of being calm?
That's wonderful, boy. Calmness is a precious quality that can have a profound impact on ourselves and those around us. Here's what Krishna told Arjuna about being calm during The Mahabharata:

yatanto yoginas cainam pasyanty atmany avasthitam
yatanto 'py akrtatmano nainam pasyanty acetasah
|| 11 ||
Striving yogis too are able to realize the soul enshrined in the body. However, those whose minds are not purified cannot cognize it, even though they strive to do so.

This shloka encourages us to strive for a calm and receptive mind in contrast to a scattered and restless one. This self-discipline, patience, and focused awareness helps one to perceive true self and gain a deeper understanding of the world around us.
So, being calm helps us understand ourselves better?
Yes, Boy. When the minc is calm, it becomes a clear mirror to our inner self. It allows us to see things as they are and understand our thoughts, emotions, and actions with clarity.
I felt really good spending time with the underprivileged kid. I want to learn how to be calm like him.
That's a beautifu intention, Boy. Cultivating calmness takes practice, just like any other skill. Techniques like yoga, meditation, deep breathing, and mindfulness can help you develop this quality over time.
I'll try my best to be calm and learn to see things clearly.

Adhyaya 16
Guruji, today I was thinking about those boys who treated Ethan badly. It's just so puzzling to me, why do people sometimes do such bad things?
Your question is important, Boy. It reminds me of a shloka.

dambho darpo 'bhimānaśh cha krodhaḥ pāruṣhyam eva cha
ajñānaṁ chābhijātasya pārtha sampadam āsurīm
|| 4 ||
O Parth, the qualities of those who possess a demoniac nature are hypocrisy, arrogance, conceit, anger, harshness, and ignorance.

So, these qualities make people do bad actions?
Yes, Boy. When these negative qualities dominate someone's behavior, they can lead to actions that harm others. Hypocrisy makes them pretend to be what they are not, arrogance and conceit blind them to the feelings of others. Anger and harshness cloud their judgment., and iIgnorance keeps them from understanding the consequences of their actions.
It sounds like these qualities create a lot of negativity.
Indeed, Boy. That's why it's important for us to cultivate positive qualities like humility, empathy, patience, and understanding. When we focus on such virtues, we can create a more harmonious and compassionate world around us.
Thank you for teaching this to me, Guruji!

Guruji, I was thinking about those boys again. What actually happens to people who have those bad qualities? And do I need to be worried about any consequences myself?
According to the Bhagavad Gita, there are two sets of qualities - divine and demoniac. The divine qualities lead to liberation, while the demoniac qualities continue to bind a person to a cycle of negative consequences.

So, those boys with bad qualities might face negative consequences?
Yes, Boy. People who exhibit qualities like hypocrisy, arrogance, anger, and more, may find themselves facing challenges and hardships in life. These qualities create disharmony and suffering not only for them but also for those around them.

And what about me, Guruji? Do I need to be worried?
There's no need to worry, my dear. Your concern for others, your desire to learn, and your curiosity about righteousness show that you possess divine qualities. Here's a shloka from The Bhagavad Gita to reassure that you were born with saintly values, and you're on the path of positivity and growth.
daivī sampad vimokṣhāya nibandhāyāsurī matā
mā śhuchaḥ sampadaṁ daivīm abhijāto 'si pāṇḍava
|| 5 ||
The divine qualities lead to liberation, while the demoniac qualities are the cause for a continuing destiny of bondage. Grieve not, O Arjun, as you were born with saintly virtues.
That's a relief, Guruji. I will continue cultivating positive qualities and focusing on the right actions.

Guruji, do people with those bad qualities pose any danger to society?
Yes, Boy. According to the Bhagavad Gita, individuals who possess negative qualities and misguided beliefs can indeed be a threat to society.

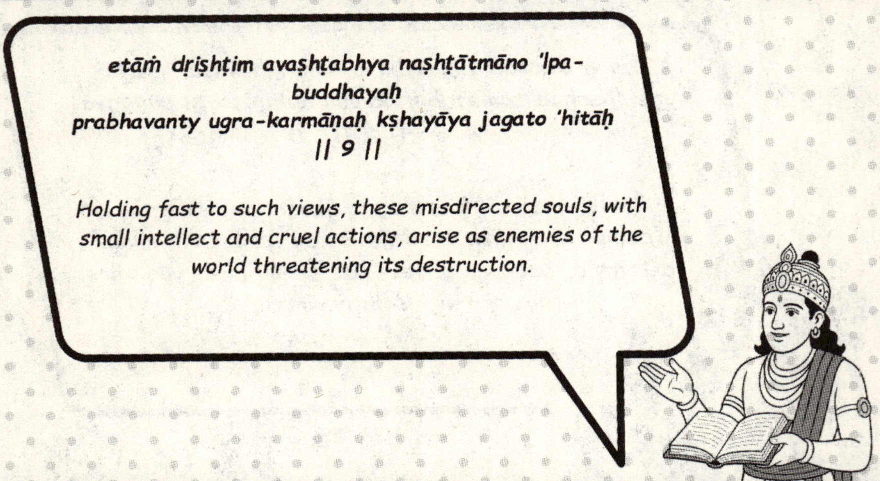
etāṁ dṛiṣhṭim avaṣhṭabhya naṣhṭātmāno 'lpa-buddhayaḥ
prabhavanty ugra-karmāṇaḥ kṣhayāya jagato 'hitāḥ
|| 9 ||
Holding fast to such views, these misdirected souls, with small intellect and cruel actions, arise as enemies of the world threatening its destruction.

The shloka explains that those with distorted views and limited understanding engage in harmful actions. Their cruel actions and negative intentions can disrupt the harmony of society and threaten its well-being.
So, their behavior can actually harm the world?

Absolutely. Their actions can lead to conflicts, divisions, and even destruction. When people act with anger, hatred, and selfishness, it creates an environment of disharmony and instability.
That's really sad, Guruji. Is there any way to prevent this?
Yes. Boy. The Bhagavad Gita guides us to cultivate positive qualities and strive for self-improvement. By choosing kindness, empathy, and wisdom, we can contribute to a more peaceful and harmonious society.
I understand, Guruji. I'll do my best to cultivate the right qualities.
That's the spirit, Boy. Your commitment to goodness will not only benefit you but also contribute to a better world for everyone.

Guruji, what happens to those with bad qualities? Do they find contentment?
No, Boy. According to the Bhagavad Gita, individuals with negative qualities often find themselves trapped in endless anxieties and desires.
So, they are not happy even when they fulfill their desires?
That's correct. Here's a shloka from The Bhagavad Gita that desires and worries persist until the end of their lives.
chintām aparimeyāṁ cha pralayāntām
upāśhritāḥ
kāmopabhoga-paramā etāvad iti niśhchitāḥ
|| 11 ||
They are obsessed with endless anxieties that end only with death. Still, they maintain with complete assurance that gratification of desires and accumulation of wealth is the highest purpose of life.

Such people are convinced that accumulating material possessions is the ultimate purpose of life. However, this pursuit only leads to temporary gratification and perpetuates their cycle of worries. This is why the Bhagavad Gita encourages us to seek higher goals beyond material desires and to cultivate qualities that lead to inner peace and lasting contentment.
I'll remember that, Guruji. It's important to find true happiness within ourselves.

Thank you for teaching this, Guruji.
I'll definitely try it the next time I get distracted!

Guruji, if someone wants to leave the path of ignorance and walk on the path of wisdom and goodness, how can they do that?
The Bhagavad Gita teaches us how to make that transition. There's a shloka that explains it well.

tri-vidhaṁ narakasyedaṁ dvāraṁ nāśhanam ātmanaḥ kāmaḥ krodhas tathā lobhas tasmād etat trayaṁ tyajet
|| 21 ||
There are three gates leading to the hell of self-destruction for the soul—lust, anger, and greed. Therefore, one should abandon all three.

So, these negative qualities keep us away from goodness?
Exactly, Boy. Lust, anger, and greed are like gates that lead us away from wisdom and goodness. They cloud our judgment, create conflicts, and make us lose sight of our true purpose. Letting go of these qualities opens the gates to goodness. Cultivating qualities like self-discipline, compassion, and selflessness leads us towards wisdom and inner peace.
It sounds like a journey, Guruji.
Indeed, Boy. It's a journey of self-discovery and growth. By recognizing and overcoming our negative tendencies, we pave the way for a more fulfilling and purposeful life.
I will remember this, Guruji. To walk on the path of wisdom, I need to leave behind lust, anger, and greed.

Adhyaya 17
Guruji, today my dad bought leafy vegetables and said they're nourishing and good for health. What kind of foods are these?
Leafy vegetables are indeed considered nourishing and healthy, my dear. They fall under the category of sattvic foods.

Sattvic foods? What does that mean, Guruji?
Sattvic foods are those that promote purity, balance, and well-being in both the body and the mind. They are foods that are full of life force and vitality. According to The Bhagavad Gita, these foods are beneficial for our physical health as well as our spiritual growth.

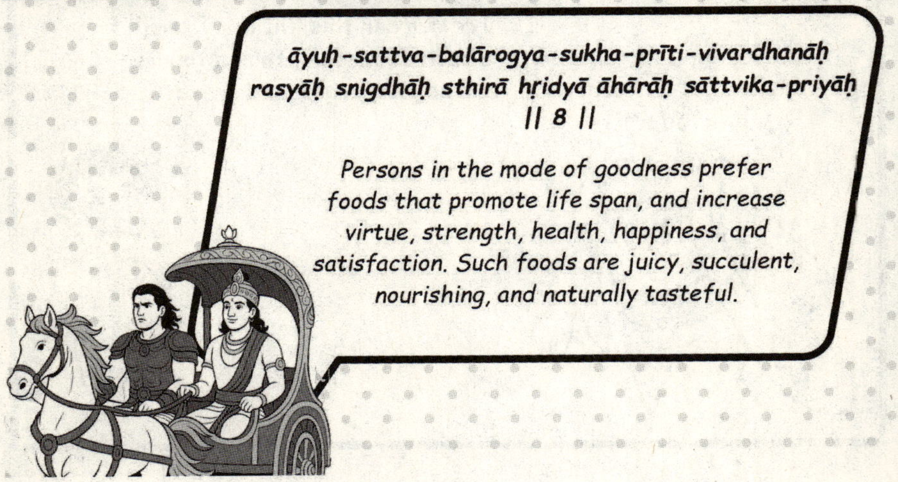
āyuḥ-sattva-balārogya-sukha-prīti-vivardhanāḥ
rasyāḥ snigdhāḥ sthirā hṛidyā āhārāḥ sāttvika-priyāḥ
|| 8 ||
Persons in the mode of goodness prefer foods that promote life span, and increase virtue, strength, health, happiness, and satisfaction. Such foods are juicy, succulent, nourishing, and naturally tasteful.

Sattvic foods are typically fresh, light, and easy to digest. These foods are not only nourishing but also promote life span, and increase virtue, strength, health, happiness, and satisfaction.
So, why are sattvic foods considered better?

Sattvic foods are believed to have a positive impact on both our body and mind. They are said to promote longevity, increase our vitality, enhance mental clarity, and create a sense of inner peace. Such foods are not just good for our physical health but also help in maintaining a calm and balanced state of mind.
I think I understand, Guruji. I'll remember to include more sattvic foods in my diet.

Guruji, you mentioned sattvic foods earlier. Are there any other kinds of foods?
Yes, my dear. There are also rajasic foods. These are quite different from sattvic foods and have a different impact on our body and mind.
Here's a shloka from The Bhagavad Gita to help you understand this better.
kaṭv-amla-lavaṇāty-uṣhṇa- tīkṣhṇa-rūkṣha-vidāhinaḥ
āhārā rājasasyeṣhṭā duḥkha-śhokāmaya-pradāḥ
|| 9 ||
Foods that are too bitter, too sour, salty, very hot, pungent, dry, and full of chillies, are dear to persons in the mode of passion. Such foods produce pain, grief, and disease.
Rajasic foods are those that are more intense and stimulating in nature. They are usually spicy, salty, sour, and even excessively hot or pungent. These foods can include things like strong spices, too much salt, and foods with lots of chili peppers.
Why are these foods considered rajasic, Guruji?

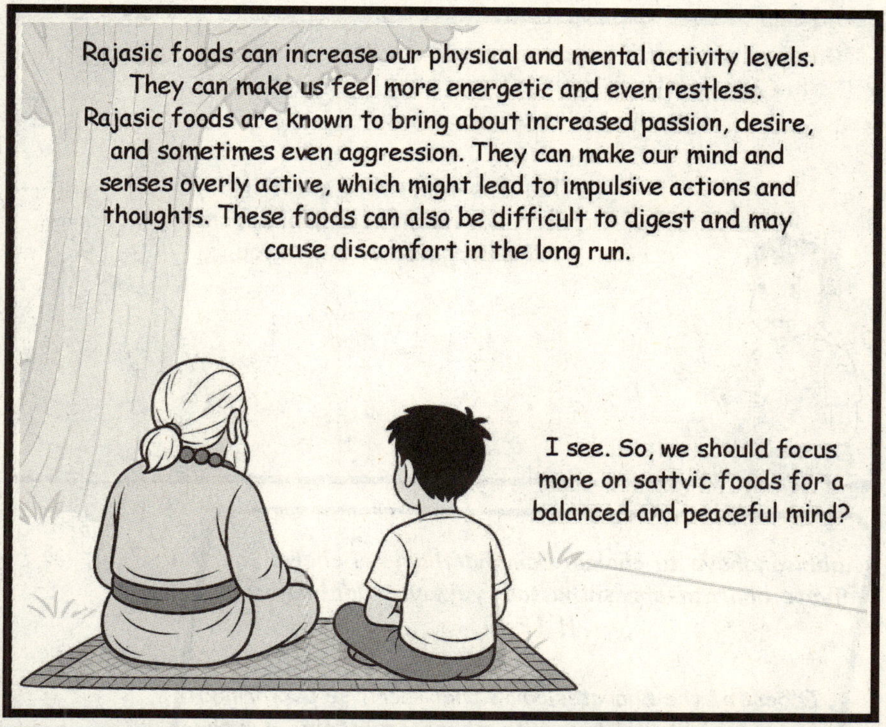
Rajasic foods can increase our physical and mental activity levels. They can make us feel more energetic and even restless. Rajasic foods are known to bring about increased passion, desire, and sometimes even aggression. They can make our mind and senses overly active, which might lead to impulsive actions and thoughts. These foods can also be difficult to digest and may cause discomfort in the long run.
I see. So, we should focus more on sattvic foods for a balanced and peaceful mind?

Exactly. Sattvic foods are known to have a calming and harmonizing effect on our body and mind. They are nourishing and promote well-being in all aspects. But remember, making conscious choices and being aware of how different foods affect you is what truly matters.
Thank you, Guruji. I'll keep this in mind and make better choices for my well-being.

Guruji, when people go to the temple and offer things to God, like flowers or food, is it okay to expect something in return from God?
That's an interesting question, my dear. Let me share a shloka from The Bhagavad Gita with you.
abhisandhāya tu phalaṁ dambhārtham api chaiva yat
ijyate bharata-śhreṣhṭha taṁ yajñaṁ viddhi rājasam
|| 12 ||
O best of the Bharatas, know that sacrifice performed for material benefit, or with a hypocritical aim, is in the mode of passion.
It says that when a sacrifice is performed with the aim of getting something in return, or when it's done with a sense of hypocrisy or showing off, then it's considered to be in the mode of passion.
Mode of passion? What does that mean?

It means that such actions are driven by desires, ego, and attachment to the outcomes. It's like doing something with a hidden agenda or expecting rewards in return.
So, is it not right to offer something to God with a wish in our heart?
It's not that it's entirely wrong, my dear. Offering things to God is an act of devotion and can be a beautiful way to express our gratitude and love. However, the essence lies in the intention behind it. If we're offering sincerely out of love and gratitude, without expecting anything in return, that's the purest form of devotion.
I understand, Guruji. So, it's like we should offer with an open heart, without any strings attached.
Exactly! Offering with love and selflessness brings us closer to the divine. It's a way of connecting with the spiritual, not just material. It's about giving without expecting, loving without conditions, and serving with humility.

Guruji, you mentioned that we should not pray with hypocrisy. But then, how should people pray? What's the right way?
It's wonderful that you're eager to learn, my dear. Let me guide you through the essence of a shloka.
deva-dwija-guru-prājña- pūjanaṁ śhaucham ārjavam
brahmacharyam ahinsā cha śhārīraṁ tapa uchyate || 14 ||
When worship of the Supreme Lord, the Brahmins, the spiritual master, the wise, and the elders is done with the observance of cleanliness, simplicity, celibacy, and non-violence then this worship is declared as the austerity of the body.
It says that when we worship the Supreme Lord, Brahmins, spiritual guides, the wise, and elders with a pure heart, along with practicing cleanliness, simplicity, celibacy, and non-violence, then that form of worship is like an austerity of the body.
Austerity of the body? What does that mean?

It means living a life of purity, simplicity, and self-discipline. When we pray with sincerity and practice virtues like cleanliness, simplicity in our actions, maintaining a celibate and focused mind, and showing non-violence in our thoughts and deeds, then that becomes a form of worship in itself.
So, it's about living a good and disciplined life?

Exactly! When we embody these virtues in our daily lives, our actions become a form of devotion. It's like showing our love and respect for the divine through our thoughts and deeds.
Thank you, Guruji. I'll remember this when I pray.

Guruji, when we pray to God, what should we say? And how should we speak when we're talking to people?
When we pray, our words should reflect our sincere intentions. There's a shloka that beautifully explains how our speech should be when we're praying to God.
anudvega-karaṁ vākyaṁ satyaṁ priya-hitaṁ cha yat
svādhyāyābhyasanaṁ chaiva vāṅ-mayaṁ tapa uchyate
|| 15||
Words that do not cause distress, are truthful, inoffensive, and beneficial, as well as regular recitation of the Vedic scriptures—these are declared as austerity of speech.
It says that our words should be gentle, not causing any distress. They should be truthful, kind, and beneficial to others. And when we engage in the regular recitation and study of sacred scriptures, that too is considered a form of austerity of speech.
Austerity of speech? What does that mean?

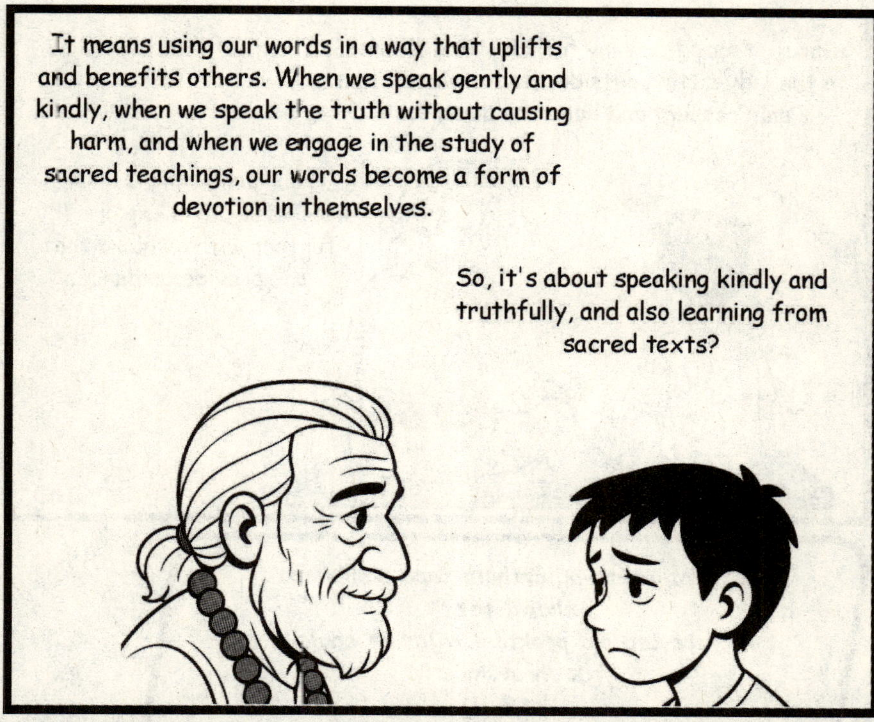
It means using our words in a way that uplifts and benefits others. When we speak gently and kindly, when we speak the truth without causing harm, and when we engage in the study of sacred teachings, our words become a form of devotion in themselves.
So, it's about speaking kindly and truthfully, and also learning from sacred texts?

Exactly! When we communicate with love and sincerity, and when we also seek wisdom from the teachings of great souls, our speech becomes a reflection of our devotion and understanding.
Thank you, Guruji. I'll remember this when I talk to people and when I pray.

Guruji, today I saw my father giving clothes to the lady sitting outside the temple. Will he gain respect and honor by doing so?
Your pondering is quite insightful. Let's explore this further with a shloka that can provide guidance.
satkāra-māna-pūjārthaṁ tapo dambhena chaiva yat
kriyate tad iha proktaṁ rājasaṁ chalam adhruvam
|| 18 ||
Austerity that is performed with ostentation for the sake of gaining honor, respect, and adoration is in the mode of passion. Its benefits are unstable and transitory.

This shloka teaches us that performing actions with the sole purpose of gaining respect, honor, or admiration falls into the category of rajasic behavior.
So, if someone does a good deed just to get respect, it's not a truly selfless act?
Exactly. When we engage in acts of kindness with the intention of seeking recognition, it taints the purity of the action.
Does that mean the benefits are temporary?
Yes, the shloka exp ains that such actions yield transient and unstable results. True selflessness lies in doing good without expecting anything in return.
Thank you, Guruji. I understand now that true goodness comes from the heart, not from the desire for recognition.

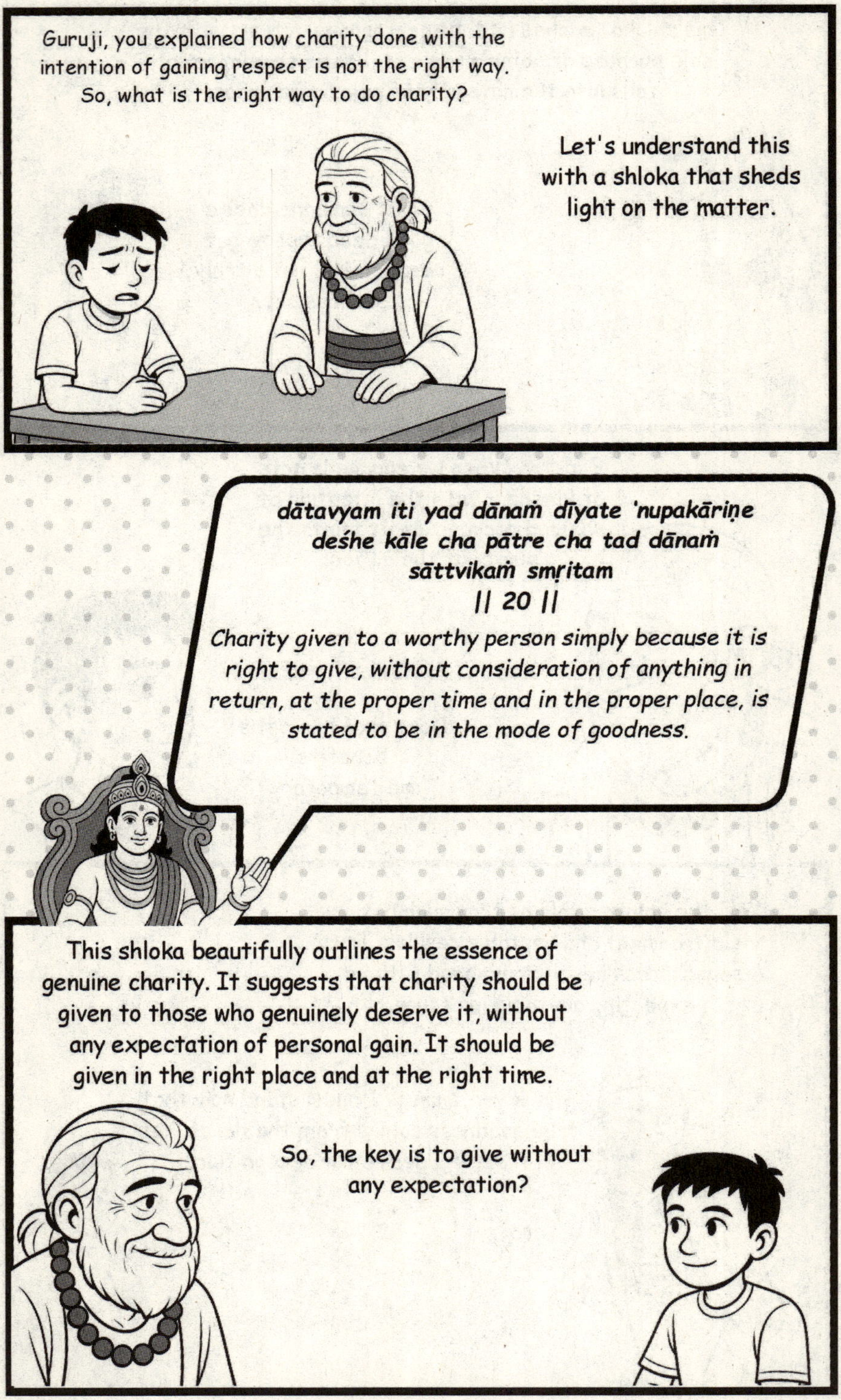
Guruji, you explained how charity done with the intention of gaining respect is not the right way. So, what is the right way to do charity?
Let's understand this with a shloka that sheds light on the matter.
dātavyam iti yad dānaṁ dīyate 'nupakāriṇe
deśhe kāle cha pātre cha tad dānaṁ
sāttvikaṁ smṛitam
|| 20 ||
Charity given to a worthy person simply because it is right to give, without consideration of anything in return, at the proper time and in the proper place, is stated to be in the mode of goodness.
This shloka beautifully outlines the essence of genuine charity. It suggests that charity should be given to those who genuinely deserve it, without any expectation of personal gain. It should be given in the right place and at the right time.
So, the key is to give without any expectation?

Exactly. The essence of true charity lies in selflessness. It's about helping those in need because it's the right thing to do, not because of what you might receive in return.
What about the proper place and time?

The shloka highlights the importance of giving charity in a way that maximizes its positive impact. Giving to the right person, at the right time, and in the right place ensures that your generosity is effective and meaningful.
Thank you, Guruji. So, true charity is about helping without expecting anything and making sure it benefits the most.

Guruji, I've been learning about charity and sacrifice. But where did these concepts originate from?
Let me share a shloka that sheds light on the origin of these profound concepts.

oṁ tat sad iti nirdeśho brahmaṇas tri-vidhaḥ smṛitaḥ
brāhmaṇās tena vedāśh cha yajñāśh cha vihitāḥ purā
|| 23 ||
The words "Om Tat Sat" have been declared as symbolic representations of the Supreme Absolute Truth, from the beginning of creation. From them came the priests, scriptures, and sacrifice.

So, the concept of sacrifice and charity is deeply rooted in the essence of creation itself?
Yes, indeed. The act of giving, of making offerings, and of engaging in selfless service is an intrinsic part of the cosmic order. It's a reflection of the divine harmony that sustains the universe.
So, when we engage in acts of charity and sacrifice, we're actually participating in something ancient and sacred.
Precisely. When you perform acts of kindness, charity, and selfless service, you're aligning yourself with the ancient rhythm of creation. You're not just giving to others; you're connecting with the universal flow of love and compassion.
Thank you, Guruji. This helps me understand that these concepts are more than just actions; they're deeply spiritual and connected to the very essence of existence.

Adhyaya 18
Guruji, today my father asked me to donate my old books to someone in need, and I did. But I'm wondering, till what age should I continue performing acts of charity?
The Bhagavad Gita has guidance for this too. There's a shloka that explains it.

Yajna-dana-tapah-karma na tyajyam karyam eva tat
yajno danam tapas caiva pavanani manisinam
|| 5 ||
Actions based upon sacrifice, charity, and penance should never be abandoned; they must certainly be performed. Indeed, acts of sacrifice, charity, and penance are purifying even for those who are wise.

It means that acts of sacrifice, charity, and penance should not be given up, but should be performed. Indeed, these acts purify even the great souls.
So, I should keep donating throughout my life?
Absolutely. The act of giving, whether it's through charity, kindness, or self-discipline, should be a consistent practice. It's not limited to a specific age. By giving to others, you not only help them but also uplift your own soul.
I will keep this in my heart, Guruji. I'll make sure to continue donating and doing good deeds throughout my life.

Guruji, today I saw a sadhu sitting outside the temple. He looked so peaceful and detached from the world. How easy is it to give up all the material pleasures and live like that?
That's a thoughtful question, Boy. The Bhagavad Gita has something to say about this very topic.
na hi deha-bhrta sakyam tyaktum karmany asesatah
yas tu karma-phala-tyagi sa tyagity abhidhiyate
|| 11 ||
For the embodied being, it is impossible to give up activities entirely. But those who relinquish the fruits of their actions are said to be truly renounced.
It means that it is indeed impossible for an embodied being to give up all activities. Therefore, the one who renounces the fruits of action is the one who has truly renounced.
So, it's not about giving up everything?

Exactly. Completely renouncing all activities while living in this world is not feasible for most people. We have duties and responsibilities towards our families, society, and ourselves. The essence lies in renouncing the attachment to the results of our actions.
Like doing things without expecting something in return?

Yes, exactly. When you perform actions with sincerity and dedication, without being attached to the outcomes, you're practicing a form of renunciation. You're letting go of the desires and the need for personal gain. This mental attitude is what leads to true inner freedom and detachment. It's about finding a balance between our worldly responsibilities and our inner growth.
Thank you, Guruji. This helps me understand better.

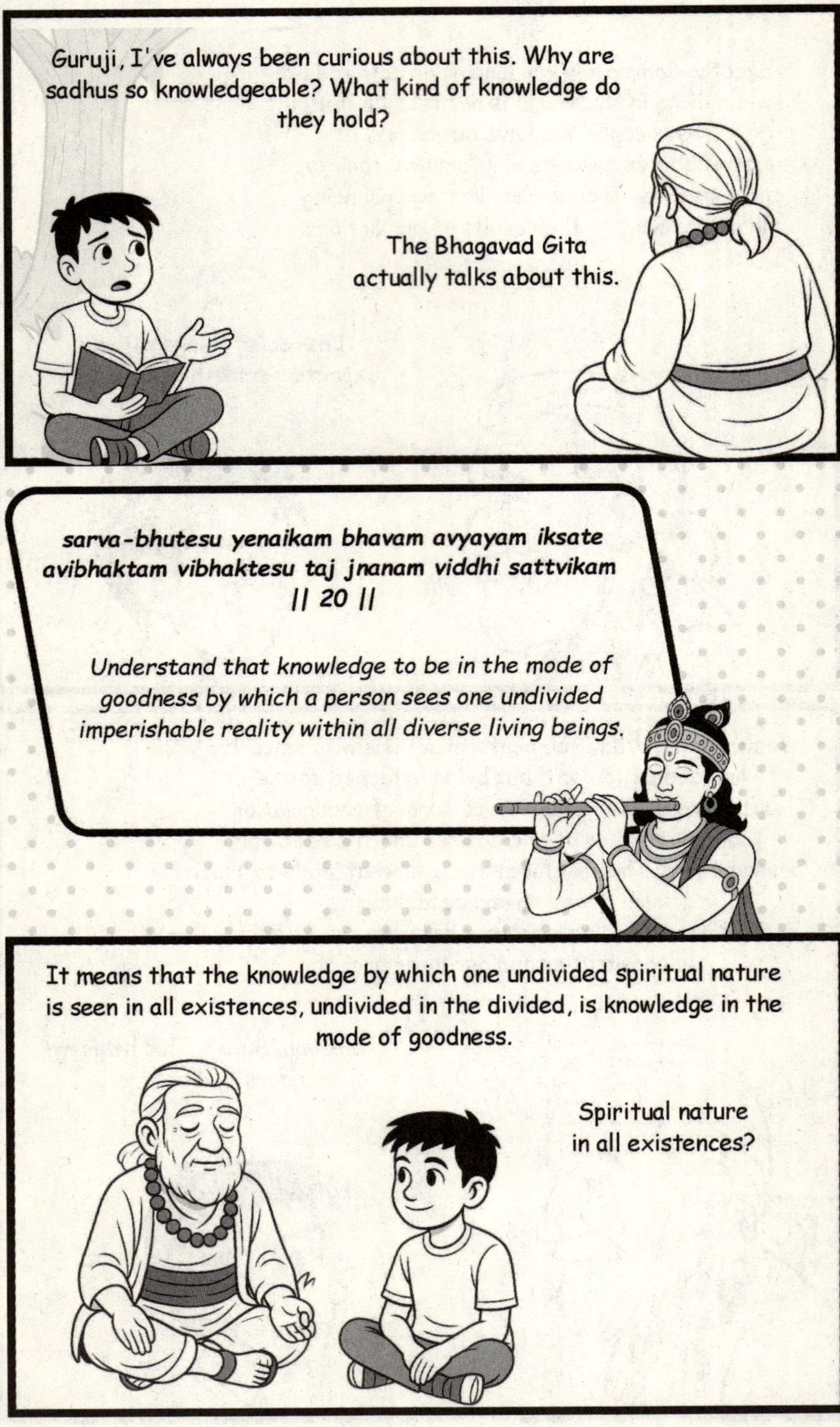
Guruji, I've always been curious about this. Why are sadhus so knowledgeable? What kind of knowledge do they hold?
The Bhagavad Gita actually talks about this.
sarva-bhutesu yenaikam bhavam avyayam iksate avibhaktam vibhaktesu taj jnanam viddhi sattvikam || 20 ||
Understand that knowledge to be in the mode of goodness by which a person sees one undivided imperishable reality within all diverse living beings.
It means that the knowledge by which one undivided spiritual nature is seen in all existences, undivided in the divided, is knowledge in the mode of goodness.
Spiritual nature in all existences?

Yes. Sadhus and enlightened beings have a deep understanding of the interconnectedness of all life forms. They see the same divine essence present in everyone and everything. This perspective comes from their profound realization and spiritual experiences.
So, they see the unity behind the diversity?
Exactly. They transcend the limitations of the physical world and perceive the underlying unity. They see that the divisions we perceive are superficial and that there's a greater reality beyond them. This kind of knowledge is rooted in purity, clarity, and a deep sense of compassion. It helps them guide others toward understanding their true nature and finding inner peace.
I guess that's why they seem so wise and calm.
Absolutely. Their wisdom comes from a place of unity, compassion, and selflessness. And remember, Boy, while we may not all become sadhus, we can cultivate this kind of knowledge by developing empathy, practicing self-awareness, and seeking a deeper understanding of life.
Thank you, Guruji. This helps me see things in a new light.

Guruji, I've been thinking about something. If gaining knowledge and inner peace brings happiness, then why do many people struggle to achieve it?
You see, happiness can sometimes be misunderstood. There's a shloka that goes like this:

Yat tad agre visam iva pariname 'mrutopamam;
Tatsukham sattvikam proktam atma-buddhi-prasada-jam.
|| 37 ||
That which seems like poison at first, but tastes like nectar in the end, is said to be happiness in the mode of goodness. It is generated by the pure intellect that is situated in self-knowledge.

It means that happiness which seems like poison at first but tastes like nectar in the end, born of clear understanding, is considered to be of the nature of goodness.
So, sometimes, the path to happiness might not seem pleasant initially?
Exactly. The journey toward true happiness often involves challenges, introspection, and sometimes facing our own shortcomings. At first, it might feel difficult or uncomfortable, just like how medicine might taste bitter but brings healing.
So, that's why people choose temporary pleasures over lasting happiness?
Yes, that's one way to put it. Sometimes, people get attached to short-term pleasures and avoid the discomfort that comes with personal growth and se f-discovery.
Thank you, Guruji. This helps me understand why some people might not see the value right away.

Guruji, I've been wondering, does God reside even in the hearts of those who are ignorant or do wrong things?
There's a shloka from The Bhagavad Gita that addresses this.

isvarah sarva-bhutanam hrd-dese 'rjuna tisthati
bhramayan sarva-bhutani yantrarudhani mayaya
|| 61 ||
The Supreme Lord dwells in the hearts of all living beings, O Arjun. According to their karmas, He directs the wanderings of the souls, who are seated on a machine made of material energy.

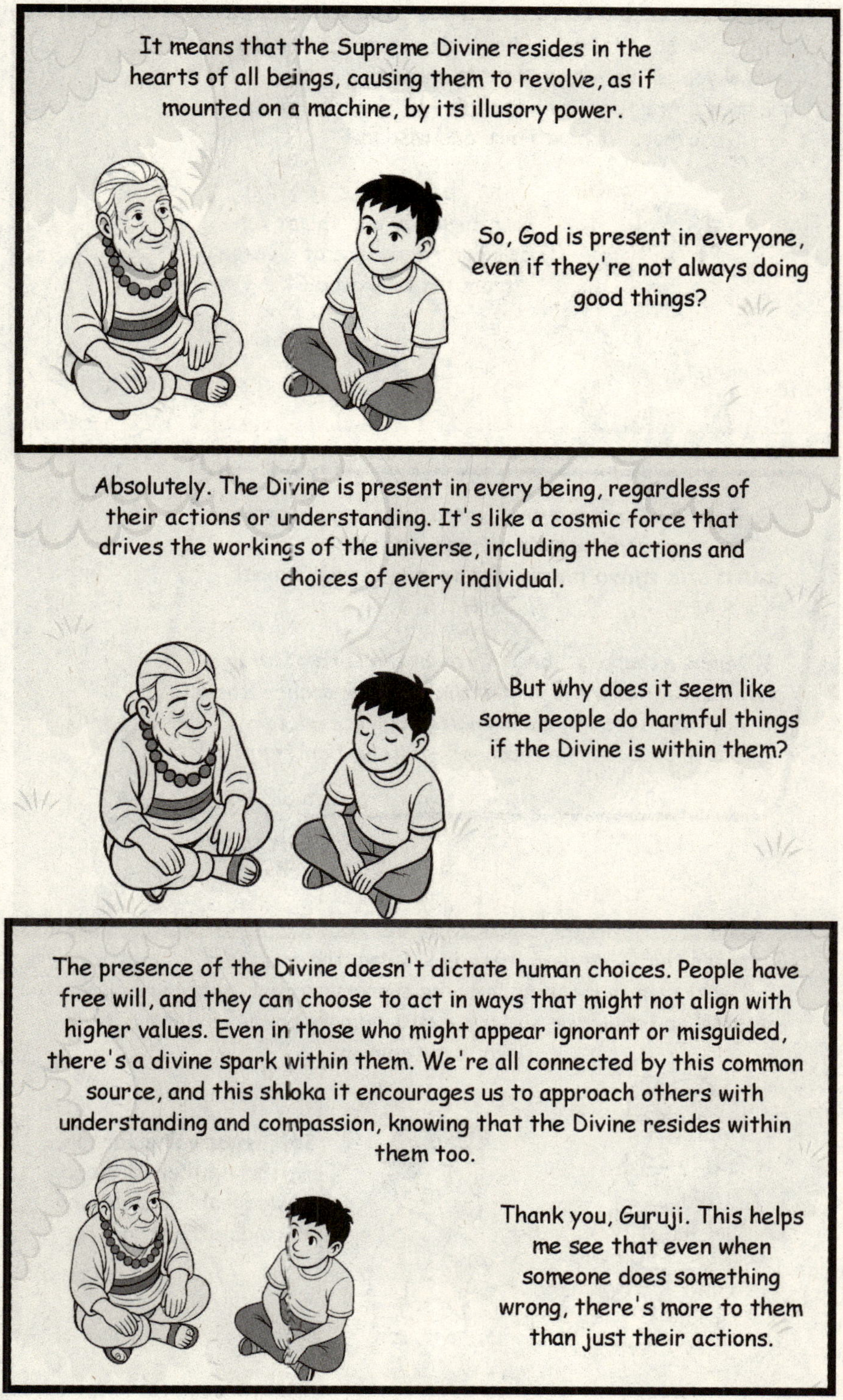
It means that the Supreme Divine resides in the hearts of all beings, causing them to revolve, as if mounted on a machine, by its illusory power.
So, God is present in everyone, even if they're not always doing good things?
Absolutely. The Divine is present in every being, regardless of their actions or understanding. It's like a cosmic force that drives the workings of the universe, including the actions and choices of every individual.
But why does it seem like some people do harmful things if the Divine is within them?
The presence of the Divine doesn't dictate human choices. People have free will, and they can choose to act in ways that might not align with higher values. Even in those who might appear ignorant or misguided, there's a divine spark within them. We're all connected by this common source, and this shloka it encourages us to approach others with understanding and compassion, knowing that the Divine resides within them too.
Thank you, Guruji. This helps me see that even when someone does something wrong, there's more to them than just their actions.

Guruji, I've been thinking about our conversations and how you've been so patient in answering all my questions. Are there more people like you who guide others with patience and wisdom?
Your curiosity and thirst for knowledge remind me of a verse from the Bhagavad Gita.
Sanjaya to Dhritrashtra: yatra yogesvarah krsno
yatra partho dhanur-dharah
tatra srir vijayo bhutir dhruva nitir matir mama
|| 78 ||
Wherever there is Shree Krishna, the Lord of all Yog, and wherever there is Arjun, the supreme archer, there will also certainly be unending opulence, victory, prosperity, and righteousness. Of this, I am certain.
It means that wherever there is Krishna, the master of all mystics, and wherever there is Arjuna, the supreme archer, there will also certainly be opulence, victory, extraordinary power, and morality. That is my opinion.
So, just as you guide me, are there other wise and knowledgeable people who guide others too?

Indeed, Boy. Just as Krishna and Arjuna in the verse symbolize the embodiment of righteousness, there are countless souls who strive to share their wisdom, inspire, and make the world a better place.
That's reassuring to know. So, these guides bring positivity and wisdom wherever they go?
Yes, just as the verse suggests, their presence brings about positive influences like opulence, victory, and morality. These guides often possess a deep understanding of life's complexities and offer insights that help people navigate challenges, find purpose, and lead more meaningful lives.
It's heartening to think that there are many sources of guidance and wisdom in the world.

Indeed, Boy. As you continue your journey through life, you'll encounter different sources of wisdom and guidance. Remember to approach them with an open heart and a discerning mind, and you'll surely find valuable lessons and insights that can enrich your life.
Thank you, Guruji. Your guidance has been so valuable to me.

It's been my pleasure to share these conversations with you, Boy. Keep seeking knowledge and exploring the depths of understanding. You'll find that the journey itself is as rewarding as the destination.